CRICUT

FOR BEGINNERS

Amanda Vinyl

© Copyright 2020 - All rights reserved.

Table of Contents

CHAPTER 1:

What is Cricut

The Cricut Machine is a plotter that can both cut various materials and write/draw on them, it can also perforate them (create those tear lines typical of cinema tickets, so to speak), engrave them (for example, Plexiglas and aluminum), create reliefs (such as in the case of embossing, even if in this house it is actually a debossing) or even folding lines (very useful if you make cards, tickets, boxes, etc.).

The machine will do one or the other depending on the accessory (blade, tip, or pen) that we are using. This machine is the Rolls Royce of cutting machines. And for good reason! Imagine any media up to 3mm thick; the machine will cut it with ten times the power of the Cricut Explore and its other competitors. What made me fall for this machine is the possibility of cutting leather.

The Cricut machine can cut cardboard, balsa, vinyl, flex, burlap (!)… And FABRIC. Yes! You read that right fabric! And not just cotton! No, all kinds of fabric imaginable! In the Design Space, you can find all kinds of fabrics: velvet, jersey, silk, lace! In all, the Maker cuts around 100 different materials up to 3mm thick. Another important feature of the Maker: you can write with it!

Whatever the type of material we want to work with the maker (paper, wood, jeans …), we will have to introduce it in the machine after making it adhere on special reusable mats, mats that are equipped with a more or less resistant layer of glue: if we are using paper we will use a mat with a layer of not very resistant glue, if we are using wood we will use a mat with a much more powerful layer of glue. There are four mats available:

1. light blue (Light Grip Mat), ideal for standard paper, light cardboard, and parchment

2. Green (Standard Grip Mat), suitable for heavy cardstock, printed paper, vinyl, and iron-on vinyl.

3. purple (Strong Grip Mat), to be used with special cardboard, chipboard, cardboard, and other heavy materials and

4. Pink (Fabric Grip) to be used with most fabrics, including cotton, polyester, denim, felt, and canvas.

The Cricut machine has a double carriage allowing two operations to be carried out in a single pass. Thus, it is possible to draw (or use the "scoring tool "to make folds) and cut at the same time.

As on the Cricut Explore, an optical drive allows for Print & Cut. However, this has been improved because it is now possible to perform a Print & Cut on colored or patterned paper.

As Cricut now favors the sale of patterns online, the Cricut Maker does not have a port to use pattern cartridges. To overcome their loyal customers' criticisms, the American brand has designed a USB adapter (sold separately) to import the patterns of the cartridges into the Design Space software.

The machine does not have an LCD screen, which can be confusing at first. But, considering that this one only displayed little on previous machines, users might think that they were limited to these few uses. Therefore, Cricut engineers decided to remove the screen to show that this machine was not limited in terms of capacity.

Cricut also emphasizes the unlimited potential of the Cricut Maker as well as its scalability. Indeed, the machine should accept in the future all future accessories that Cricut will market.

In terms of storage, we can note 2 locations for storing unused blades, pencils, or other small accessories. The Cricut Maker is rightly considered the Rolls Roys from Cricut! You will never feel like this machine limits you because of the many possibilities it can offer you. If you sew, you will no longer cry to tear your fabrics thanks to the 2 dedicated blades (rotating + special coated fabric blade). The price can be a drag for some; however, this is a tough and versatile machine that you will keep for a long time. Therefore, we must consider this as a long-term investment. The Cricut Maker is a machine that you will not disappoint and that you will use for many years to come.

CHAPTER 2:

How to Start

Guidelines to Use Cricut

The Top Panel of the Cricut Design Space

This section of the Cricut Design Space is used for correcting and coordinating components on the canvas area. This panel allows you to select your desired font and sizes; it also gives room to bring designs into line and a lot more.

The top panel of the Cricut Design Space is categorized into two sub-panels; one is to manage and revise elements on the canvas area, while the other is for saving, naming, and cutting your assignments.

Sub-Panel #1: Name and Cut Your Assignment

Sub-panel #1 is for plotting a route around your account, assignments, and cutting your finished projects.

Toggle Menu: clicking on this menu will produce another menu entirely. This menu is very practical, but it is not an element of the canvas. For this reason, there won't be a lot of information about this menu in this book. The primary use of the toggle menu is that it allows you to change your picture.

This menu also allows other functional and mechanical things like resetting your machine, blades, and firmware of your machine. It is also possible to organize your Circuit Access account and subscription. You can accomplish a lot with the toggle menu; give yourself a few hours to click on every link and option available to take full advantage of the Cricut Design Space.

The dimensions and visibility of the Canvas can be altered on the settings page; there will be more in-depth information about this in subsequent pages of this book.

Project Name

Every assignment you work on can only be named after a minimum of one component like shape, image, or any other thing you want to work with. They will all begin with the "Untitled title," so you are at liberty to save them with whatever you wish.

My Projects

Your previous works are saved under my "My projects," so clicking on it will lead you to your library of assignments. Sometimes, there may be a need to edit saved work; this will save you the stress of creating the same thing.

Save

You can work with this option after placing a minimum of one component on the canvas area. You will lose your assignments if you don't save them as you proceed. Though the software is on the cloud, don't forget that browser can crash at any time.

Maker—Explore (machine)

Your project type will dictate whether you will work with Maker, Cricut Joy, or the Cricut Explore Machine. The Cricut Maker will only provide options that suit the type of machine you are using. For instance, creating with the Explore option ON and at the same time working with a Maker is not compatible because you won't be able to activate the tools of the Maker. The alternatives are for line type.

Make It

Click on make it after the successful upload of your file, and you want to cut it. Make it option is also great for people with more than one project to cut because it allows the user to increase their assignments. The mats split your assignments based on the color of the assignment.

Sub-Panel #2 – Editing Menu

This second panel is great for editing, systematizing, and positioning images and fonts on the canvas area.

Fill and Linetype

The linetype and fill option informs your machine of the appropriate blades and tools. The machine you chose in the upper part of the window, either Explore or Maker, will not produce the same results.

Wave, Engrave, Perf, and Deboss: These are the Cricut Maker machine's latest features that can be used to produce mind-blowing effects on several materials. They are used with the Quick Swap adaptive tool; so, all you need is the tip if you have one. There is not much information on these tools because they are still new, but later, as we get familiar with them, there will more than enough tips on how to navigate them.

Edit

This option gives room for copying (which is to lift an item while leaving the original as it is), cutting (taking an item out entirely from the canvas), and pasting (dropping cut or copied items on the canvas area) elements from the canvas. Clicking on the "Edit" icon opens up a new list of menu. You can use the copy and cut selections when you have selected component(s) from the canvas area. The paste selection is activated after you cut or copy any element(s).

Linetype

The linetype option informs your machine of the type of tool you will need and the time for cutting your project. There are presently seven selections – Draw, Deboss, Perf, Engrave, Cut, Wave, and Score. All the selections are available on the Cricut Maker, but only the Score, Cut, and Draw are on the Cricut Explore.

Undo and Redo

We can't always be perfect; mistakes are sometimes bound to happen. The undo and redo buttons help to amend these faults. The undo button works when you want to erase a mistake or if the work is not satisfactory. Make use of the redo button whenever you mistakenly edited or deleted something.

Draw: Your Cricut also has an option that allows you to write on your creations. There will be a notice asking you to select from the available Cricut Pens if you go with this linetype option; this does not just work with any pen type. You need a third-party adapter; otherwise, it calls for particular pens. It bears mentioning that this line type option cannot give the colors to your design.

The layers on the canvas area will be sketched out with the selected pen color after picking the desired design. When working with this option, the Cricut will draw or write when you select "Make it."

Cut: Every element on the canvas has "Cut" as the standard linetype, implying that your machine will cut the designs when you click on "Make it." You can alter the fill of the components on the canvas area with the "Cut" button. This variation will lead to a different color of materials for cutting your projects.

Score: This option is similar to the scoring line, though it is more efficient. Employing this linetype selection to design will make it look dashed or lined. Clicking on "Make it" when using the scoring option will not cut your materials but score them. This process requires using a scoring wheel or scoring stylus; however, the scoring wheel is only compatible with the Cricut Maker.

Fill

This selection is majorly for patterns and printing. It won't work unless you have the "Cut" option as a linetype. "No Fill" implies that the user can't print anything.

Print: I think that this is the most fascinating option that Cricut has to offer. This feature is for printing designs and then cut them. After activating the fill selection, click on "Make it," then send the files to your printer. You can leave the Cricut to do its thing, which is to cut.

The print option also allows the user to add patterns to any type of layer. You can either use your patterns or the ones made available by Cricut. You can go as far as your imagination can take you when adding patterns to layers. For instance, you can create a stunning card with a ready-made pattern from Cricut Access, which of course, you have to pay for, or your designs. Then, print and cut your card at once.

Select All

The "Select all" option simplifies moving all your components to the canvas area; it relieves you of the trouble of selecting the elements one by one.

Align

Anyone who can get their way around other graphic design programs can work with this option. You must have a full understanding of the usage of "Align" tools to get the best out of your Cricut experience. The align menu is comprehensive, but the major things you need to know are summarized below:

Align

This is the option that lets the user put all their creations in a straight line. It starts to work after selecting two or more components on the canvas area.

Align Left

This works just like the "Align Right," except that the components will be moved to the left, depending on the component that is at the farthest left.

Align Right

This option makes your entire element parallel to the right according to the component that is at the farthest right.

Align Top

As in the "Align Bottom," the components will be brought into line at the top according to the element that is at the extreme top.

Align Bottom

When this setting is activated, every selected element will be moved to the bottom in a straight line. The component at the far end at the base will order the direction of other elements.

Distribute

The "Distribute" option will enable precise, fast, uniform spacing between the components. It won't work unless there is a minimum of three components selected.

Distribute Vertically

Clicking on this selection will distribute the components vertically. The elements at the extreme top and base of the dictate how long the distribution will be. This implies that the middle elements will be distributed between the top and base elements.

Distribute Horizontally

This works just like the "Distribute Vertically" option except that the elements will be distributed horizontally, and the elements on the far right and left will order the length of the distribution. The items in the middle are also distributed between the right and left elements.

Arrange

Whenever you add new designs to the canvas, if you are dealing with several images, each one you add will be in front of the previously added ones. There may be a need to reposition some of the designs to the front or the back; this is where the "Arrange" option comes in to save the day. One of the great features of this option is that the program can tell each design's position with a click. The Design Space will then make the possible options for the component available.

The possible options for arrangement are below:

o Send to front: Selecting this option will transfer the selected component to the far front.

o Send to back: This option will move the selected components to the far back.

o Move Backward: This selection will transfer the particular component a step backward. For instance, in a three-component creation, moving the first component backward will move it to the second position.

o   Move Forward: this selection moves a selected component a step forward. This option is particularly useful when working with five or more items.

Center

A click on this option will produce a captivating alignment of texts vertically and horizontally, crossing a design over another. This selection works well for someone that desires to align texts in the middle in shapes like a star or square.

Center Vertically

This selection is great for a user designing with columns and desires to arrange and make them parallel. It's a no brainer that it will straighten the components of the canvas area vertically.

Center Horizontally

When working with this setting, your images and texts will be parallel horizontally to the middle of the canvas area.

Size

There is nothing that you type or design in the Design Space that does not have a size. It is possible to alter the components' size to a precise, particular dimension with a click. The little lock plays an essential role when working with this option. After altering an image or design's size, clicking on the lock, send a message to the program that you want to discard the former measurements.

Position

This is the feature that tells you the location of your components on the canvas area. Though the tool is a bit complicated, it is practical for transferring your components from one point on the canvas area to the other by being specific about where you want them to be. The alignment tools explained above can also serve the purpose of this option.

Rotate

It is also easy to rotate a component from the canvas area, though certain designs require particular angles. If you are fussy about the angle at which you want to rotate your designs, the "Rotate" option is the best for you.

Flip

The "Flip" option is a brilliant means of reflecting any design in the Cricut Design Space. The "Flip" selection is in two parts:

Flip Horizontally

This selection produces a horizontal reflection of images or designs. It is the best feature for producing left and right designs like the ones in a mirror. For instance, if you are trying to create wings and have the right side ready, all you have to do to get the left side is to flip horizontally.

Flip Vertically

The resultant effect of this option is similar to the reflection of objects on water. It turns the designs vertically, and it is the best option for generating a shadow effect.

Font

A click on this option will change the font of your assignments; it also helps to search and filter the fonts from the upper part of the window. Anyone who works with Cricut Access can access all the fonts with a small green "A" at the font title's start. If this is not the case, the user can employ their system's font if they don't want to pay when their assignment is being cut.

Font Size Line, Letter and, Space

These options have a lot of perks, particularly the letter spacing.

Line Space

This option solves producing a text line because of irregular spacing; it ensures a uniform spacing between lines within a paragraph.

Letter Space

This option lets the user decrease the space between letters rapidly. Some fonts have too much space separating each letter.

Font Size

Though it is possible to alter the font size from the canvas area, this option also gets the job done.

Ungroup to Layers

This option is one of the most complicated ones. This function works with and available for just Multi-Layer fonts, which are only accessible in Cricut Access or personal purchase. The multi-layer font has more than one layer with colors or shadows around it. It is easy to separate the layers, select the text, and click on "Ungroup to layers," and you're done.

Alignment

This "Alignment" option is not the same as discussed earlier; this particular one is for paragraphs.

The available options for this "Alignment" are listed below:

- o   Right: this moves a paragraph to the right in a straight line.

- o Left: this option brings a paragraph in line to the left.

- o Center: it aligns a paragraph to the middle.

Style

There is the chance to alter the appearance of your selected font. The options available, but not limited to, are below:

- o Bold: this option makes the selected font thicker.

- o Regular: this is the standard form of writing that won't modify the writing system

- o Italic: this inclines the font to the right-hand side.

- o Bold italic: it makes the italic font look thicker.

Curve

This function infuses extra ingenuity into your text; it allows the user to curve a text. It is mastered by occupying yourself with the small slider. Moving the slider to the right bends the text inwards while moving it to the left will curve the text upwards. Your text will produce a circle if you move the slider completely to the right or left.

Advance

This is the option that comes last on the editing panel. The term "Advance" may seem daunting, but there is no big deal in using it when you understand what every option works for.

Ungroup to Letters

This is your go-to option if you intend to change every character; this option is to separate each letter into one layer.

Ungroup to Lines

This function is for separating paragraphs on different lines. To work with this, type the paragraph and select "Ungroup to Letters;" that is all you have to do to get the particular line you want to edit.

Starting a New Project

When starting a new project, you will want to know what that project will be and what materials you will be using before doing anything else.

For example, if you want to cut vinyl letters to place on wood, you will need to know your dimensions, so your letters fit evenly and centered on the wood. You will need wood that vinyl can adhere to without the risk of peeling. And you will want to make certain that your wood is sanded and finished to your desire because you do not want any imperfections. You may even find, with store-bought wood pieces advertised as ready-to-use, there are tiny imperfections.

When working with fabric, you want to make sure that you know what inks or types of vinyl will adhere to the surface. You do not want any peeling or cracking to happen to your beautiful design.

When working with any kind of fabric, including canvas bags, you will want to pre-wash for sizing, because shrinkage, after your design has been set, can cause the design to become distorted.

If you are not sure exactly what you want to do, have something in mind so that you are not wasting a lot of materials by trial and error. The cost of crafting materials can add up, so you will want to eliminate as much potential waste as possible.

If you are new to Cricut Design Space, start with something simple. You do not want to get in over your head. That is the worst thing you can do when you learn any new craft. Many used Cricut machines for sale, and while some users sell because they upgraded, others are users who gave up. You invested, and you will want to get a return on that investment.

The first thing that you will get when you launch the Cricut Design Space for the first time is a very quick tutorial on how to insert a shape and how to fill that shape with a colored pattern. Go ahead and run through that process a few times until you are familiar with where the various assets and options are. You can introduce a shape into the design Space, change the linetype, and change what the shape is filled with.

As the first step, we are going to select the 'Text' option. In the text box that appears, we will type the phrase, 'Good Vibes,' and pick a font in the Design Space that you like. Do remember that some of the fonts in that list will have a cost. If you are looking for free fonts exclusively, you can choose the 'System Fonts,' which are the fonts that are already installed on your computer.

Using the measurements at the top of the Design Space cut a piece of vinyl that is adequately-sized to accommodate your design. Get your light blue or light-grip Cricut Maker mat, and line up your vinyl so your design will print on it. Make adjustments to where your design is in the Design Space if you need to!

Once you have your vinyl where you need it, use the rounded back of your scraper/burnishing tool to smooth the vinyl down on the gripped surface, working from the middle out towards the edges. Ensure that the piece is lying flat with no bubbles or wrinkles, so you get the crispest and precise cuts possible.

Once the Cricut 'C' button is blinking, press it once and watch it work its magic! Once the machine has completed its cut, remove the machine's mat and bring it to your crafting space. Using the rounded back of your scraper/burnishing tool, smooth the vinyl's entire surface on your mat. This will help the carrier sheet hold onto your design parts that you do not want to weed.

Once you have thoroughly rubbed the entire piece, use your weeding tool to pick up the blanks around your letters. The background, the circles in your O and G, all the things you do not want to stick to your laptop. Once only the letters remain on the carrier sheet, cut an appropriately-sized piece of transfer tape. Using the back of your scraper, smooth the transfer tape down onto the entirety of your design. Once you have a good grip on your design, peel the tape back from the carrier sheet.

Using some rubbing alcohol, clean the space on your laptop where you intend to place your design. Once it is completely clean, lay the design where you want it and rub it into place using your scraper's back. Carefully peel back your transfer sheet to reveal your new design and admire your handiwork! You have just completed your first Cricut project!

Innovation is the catchphrase for being effective in the microstock business. To stand apart from the group and be seen, it is basic to separate yourself from the rest. The best way to do so is to consider new ideas and understand things from a better perspective. I need to impart to you three different ways by which you can fire your reasoning aptitudes and concoct progressively unique thoughts and motivations.

CHAPTER 3:

Types of Cricut

Cricut Models

The kinds of projects you plan on doing will determine the type of Cricut machine you decide to buy. Each of them is capable of specialized features, and here you will find those things out. Opt for what will meet your needs richly.

However, some things are common to all the Cricut types, and you need to know that. The three Cricut devices have Bluetooth connective technology built with them that aid easy connections with your phones and computers. They all also have a free Cricut Design Software.

Now, for distinction purposes, let us discuss the Cricut Explore Air.

Cricut Explore Air

It is a device you will find in the home of every crafter, and why is this? It is proficient enough to cut over a thousand different materials, each of varying density and texture. It also allows you to use four great tools for you to score, write, and cut.

Cricut Maker

The Cricut Maker is another great device that will help you with compassionate and discreet design projects. It can cut materials with high-density levels like wood and fabric. You will notice that that is one thing the Cricut Explore Air doesn't have. For everything you need your Cricut to do, this machine provides you access to about twelve efficient tools that spray your work with the air of professionalism.

Cricut Joy

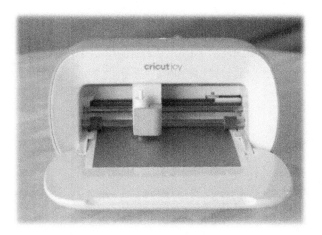

The Cricut Joy device is a newly introduced Cricut. It is relatively smaller than the other two and comes with a few more attractive features too.

Various Models

Cricut Explore Air 2

The Cricut Explore Air 2 is the following stage up from the Explore Air, and it has one significant update: Fast Mode. This is extremely useful for individuals who make various duplicates of their tasks (like educators) or individuals who make things to sell who will value the measure of time they have left over.

The Cricut Explore Air 2 accompanies the standard Fine-Point Blade, which enables you to cut several materials. It's perfect with the Deep Point Blade and the Bonded Fabric Blade (sold independently) to enable you to cut considerably more materials.

The Cricut Explore Air 2 also has worked in Bluetooth abilities to cut remotely and a double tool holder so you can cut and compose all in a solitary pass. Furthermore, similar to the Explore Air, the second clamp is good with frills like the Scoring Stylus, Cricut Pens, etc. Hence, there's no compelling reason to buy an extra connector.

I don't utilize Fast Mode all that frequently, so the progression up from the Explore Air is not a huge deal for me, however, it can spare you time if you do a ton of cardstock, vinyl, and iron-on projects!

Features:

- With Cricut Pens to make "written by hand" cards and different projects

- Cut multifaceted subtleties with extreme exactness

- With Scoring Stylus to crease cards, boxes, envelopes, acetic acid derivation and to make 3D paper specialties

- With Fast Mode for 2X quicker cutting

- You can work with more than 100+ sorts of materials

- Among the more than 370 textual styles to look over

- Can work with an Android or iOS gadget

- Remote cutting with Bluetooth

- Utilizations Design Space to deal with records from any gadget

- With Cricut Image Library

Pros:

- Scoring Stylus folds' lines for various projects

- Cuts with extreme accuracy

- Works with more than 100+ materials

- Writes more than 370 text styles

- Structure anyplace with Design Space

- Associates with gadgets utilizing Bluetooth

- Cut and write multiple times quicker

Cons:

- Issues with Design Space

- Disconnected Design Space accessible for iOS clients

Cricut Explore One

The Cricut Explore One is Circuits' entrance level spending machine; it's ideal for any individual who needs to begin with a digital die cutting machine, yet wouldn't like to spend a huge amount of cash. It accompanies the standard Fine-Point Blade, which enables you to cut several materials. It's perfect with the Deep Point Blade and the Bonded Fabric Blade (sold independently) to enable you to cut considerably more materials.

As its name suggests, the Explore One has a single apparatus holder. If you need to cut and write in a similar project, you should change the sharp edge for a pen mid-route through the cut. It's extremely simple to change out the accessory or blade. The Design Space programming will stop the slice and walk you through it when now is the right time, yet if you do a lot of tasks that join cutting, composing, or scoring, it can get tiresome sooner or later.

Moreover, really, the single tools holder is good with the standard estimated edges (Fine-Point, Deep Point, and Bonded Fabric); however, to utilize different instruments and extras, you'll have to buy a different connector to fit in the single device holder.

The Explore One doesn't have worked in Bluetooth capacities, so you need to connect the machine to your gadget with the USB link gave. Or you can also buy a Bluetooth connector independently to enable the machine to cut remotely.

Features:

- Utilize the Cricut Design Space for PC, Mac, iPad, or iPhone

- Transfer your plans for nothing or pick one from the Cricut Image Library

- Use text styles introduced from your PC

- Work on various materials from flimsy paper to thick vinyl

- With helpful device and extras holder

- Works remotely by including a remote Bluetooth connector

- No compelling reason to set with the Smart Set dial or make your very own custom settings

- Make extends in minutes

Pros:

- Works remotely with Bluetooth connector

- Transfer your very own pictures and structures for nothing

- With 50,000+ pictures and text styles from Cricut Image Library

- No settings required with the Smart Set dial

- Prints and cuts quick

- Structure with your very own gadget or PC utilizing Design Space

Cons:

- It expenses to utilize pictures beginning at $0.99

- Bluetooth connector sold independently

CHAPTER 4:

The Cricut Maker

Cricut Maker Machine

The Cricut Maker is Circuits' most up to date machine. Cricut considers it a definitive smart cutting machine, and I can't help but agree. It is a best in class digital die cutting machine that conveys proficient quality outcomes at an individual machine cost. It can cut many materials, from the most delicate fabric and paper to mat board, balsa wood, and leather.

The Cricut Maker utilizes the fresh out of the box new Adaptive Tool System, which considers progressively precise control over the instruments, including pivoting, lifting, and shifting weight all through the whole cut. The Adaptive Tool System also enables the machine to use new devices later on as Cricut grows its device contributions.

Different Parts of the Cricut Maker

The following overview of the machine starts with the machine's front from the left-hand side when sitting in front of the cutting machine.

Tool Cups

On the machine's left-hand side, there is a dual-slot for crafting tools such as a pair of scissors, tweezers, weeding tools, and so on. It has one pocket deeper than the other, each with a protective silicone base for any blades that may be stored.

Mobile Device Holder Slot

Beneath the top flap of the machine, there is a long groove that runs over the cutting machine's mouth. This slot is conveniently designed to hold a mobile device such as a phone or tablet.

Cricut Cartridge Port

The Cricut Maker machine does not come with a Cricut Cartridge port. However, it can still take cartridges with the help of a USB cartridge adaptor sold separately.

Top Lid

The top lid flips up and offers support for a mobile phone or tablet to lean against if they are inserted into the mobile device slot. It is also a protective cover for the machine when it is not in use.

Cricut Accessory and Blade Housing Head

In the mouth of the machine, you will find the Cricut accessory and blade housing head.

This head holds the accessory and blade clamps. This housing is a double tool holder, making it easier for the machine to operate dual functions such as cutting and scoring simultaneously.

This means that you do not have to change accessories halfway through a project.

This housing head moves along a housing head guide bar located a little way back from, but just above, the material feeder guide bar.

Accessory Clamp A

Accessory clamp A is for the Scoring Stylus pen and other Cricut drawing or marking pens compatible with the cutting machine.

Blade Clamp B

Blade clamp B is for blades and blade housings.

Material Feeder Guide Bar

The material feeder guide bar helps to hold the cutting mat steady. The cutting blades can glide over the material.

Feeder Guide Rollers

The feeder guide rollers are the two grey rollers located on either side of the material feeder guide bar. These rollers roll the material back and forth so that the machine can cut the materials.

Star Wheels

The star wheels are the small, white wheels that look like little stars. There are four of them, and they are located between the two grey feeder guide rollers. They help to keep the material steady during cutting. Some materials will require moving these little wheels to the one side of the bar so that they will not make indents in the material. Some material is too thick for these little wheels and could cause them damage.

Mat Guides

These are the two little plastic feet that are located in front of the gray feeder guide rollers. They are there to guide the cutting mats into position and mark the maximum cutting mat or material size that can be fed through the cutting machine.

Bottom Feeder Plate

The bottom feeder plate is the portion that the material will sit on while it is being cut and will rest upon when the cut is finished. It is also the plate that protects the machine and folds up when the machine is not in use.

Bottom Storage Drawer

The bottom storage drawer is a secret compartment that is housed in the bottom feeder plate. Here, you can store your accessories such as cutting rulers, pins, scissors, scraper, drive housings, and so on. There is a long compartment, a smaller square compartment, and two smaller ones. One of the smaller compartments contains a magnetic strip that is great for keeping blades and pins from rattling around the compartment.

Load/Unload Mat Button

On the top right-hand side of the machine at the front is the load/unload cutting mat button. This button has an up and down arrow on it to indicate load and unload. This is the button you will use to load the cutting into the machine when you are ready to cut. It is also the button that you will use to unload the cutting mat once the cutting machine has finished cutting the design.

Go Button

The Go button is located right next to the load/unload cutting mat button and is marked with a little green "C" for Cricut. This is the button that you will press when you are ready to start cutting the design.

Pause Button

At times, you may need to stop cutting for whatever reason. This is when this button comes in handy. It is located next to the go button. It is marked with two lines running next to each other, much like the pause button on any electronic gaming, TV, or DVD device.

Smart Set Dial

The Cricut Maker does not have a Smart Set dial. The material selection is chosen through the Design Space software.

Power Button

The power button is located just above the load/unload cutting mat button on the cutting machine's top.

USB Utility Port

The USB utility port is located at the bottom right-hand side of the machine. This port is used to charge mobile devices while connected via Bluetooth to the machine for cutting. It must not be confused with the USB port that is at the back of the machine, which is used to connect the machine to a computer.

USB Port

The USB port for the machine is located at the back of the machine near the power port. This is used to update the machine's firmware and to connect to a device.

Power Port

The Cricut Maker's power port is located at the back of the cutting machine.

Material Feeder Slot

The cutter cuts materials up to 12" long at one time. The cutter needs to slide the mat back and forth across the blade or any accessories loaded for the project to cut out these patterns.

That is why there is a material feeder slot at the back of the machine; so the mat can slide in and out to cut the material's full length.

Other than the Fine-Point Blade, Deep Cut Blade, and Bonded Fabric Blade that are good with all Cricut machines, the Maker can also utilize the accompanying apparatuses that are perfect with the Adaptive Tool System:

Rotating Blade – This gives you a chance to cut fabric with a Cricut Maker. It's a tremendous improvement over-utilizing the standard Fine-Point cutting edge. You can cut intense fabric like burlap or denim and delicate materials like crepe paper or glossy silk. This cutting edge gives you a chance to make intricate cuts on fabric without fraying or clustering (which is why you need a stabilizer backing when utilizing the Fine-Point blade).

Knife Blade lets you effectively cut through thicker and denser materials, such as balsa wood, leather, mat board, and Cricut Chipboard. You can make some quite complex cuts without worrying that the sharp edge will snap.

Scoring Wheels – These apparatuses make crisp creases on slender, thick, and even covered paper materials. They enable you to make extra-deep score lines on any material that doesn't break when you fold it.

The Explore machines can't utilize these new sharp edges and instruments since they depend on the Adaptive Tool System. The standard instrument holder carriage in the Explore machines simply doesn't have the necessary exactness or power.

As the name suggests, the Adaptive Tool System is intended to easily switch between devices, adjusting the drive framework to whichever device is loaded into it. This considers TONS of new kinds of instruments to be made, later on, to do new sorts of arts with the machine that we never could.

Features of the Cricut Maker

- With expandable devices: revolving cutting edge, pens, and knife blade

- With fine point pen, 12 x 12 inches cutting mats

- The rotational cutting edge can cut quickly and precisely

- Accompanies several computerized sewing designs

- The knife blade can deal with meager and thick materials

- With a simple structure application; load extends on a PC or cell phone

- With a gadget docking space

- You can utilize your own plans

- With a USB port to charge your gadget while being used

- With Bluetooth remote innovation

Pros

- Enables you to work at various materials

- You can utilize various structures from its database

- Accompanies expandable devices

- Gadget dock gives you a chance to work intimately with the machine

- Utilize your PC or cell phone with the Cricut

Cons

- Objections that it won't work with an iPad

- The blade edge is sold independently

CHAPTER 5:

Uses of Cricut Machine

Home Décor Projects

The Cricut is a machine that can allow you to create a ton of DIY projects and art designs. One of the places where you will find that the Cricut is most useful is in the area of creating home décor projects and materials you can use to spice up your living apartment. The options that exist here are too many, and they include;

- Designs from contact paper. Some of these designs include the polka dot wall design, touches on the floor coverings of houses using the contact papers of different colors, and many other things that you can think of.

- Vinyl art, which can be used to spice up just about any surface you can think of, including your child's space, the baby crib, or even the walls above your kitchen cabinets. These projects are a great way to give your living area the much-needed lived-in feeling and also to spice up the house a bit.

- 3d papercraft. Using your Cricut, you can print 3d papers of different designs and use them to design your living and working area. One of these is in the 3d flower wall treatment in which 3d forms are cut into the shape of intricately-designed flowers, and these are used on the walls of houses. There are no limits to what the artist can come up with at this point, and it is up to you to decide what you want to do with these papers. The watchword is to get creative with your craft.

Artwork Projects

There are a lot of opportunities that exist when it comes to artwork and Cricut crafts. Here are a few uses of the Cricut in this regard;

- Wall art, including Chevron designs on canvas, bespoke designs made on frames, etc.

- Comfortable swap gallery frames that can be used to collate your best piece of artwork and pictures for easy referencing, etc.

- Typography artwork where the pieces that have been created from the Cricut are used to spell out words and pass messages across, especially on plain surfaces.

Home Décor Accessories

There are also a ton of possibilities that exist here. In this category, pieces that are cut from the Cricut machine are used to make intricate and sometimes plain designs on accessories that are in the house of the owner. Just as is the case with the other projects, there is no limit to what the artist or the person carrying out the project can achieve; it is all dependent on what he wants to achieve and how creative he can allow himself to become. A few classical examples of what you can earn or the designs you can create under this category include;

- Monogrammed memo boards, where the Cricut pieces are used to design memo boards to make them more attractive and fun to be interacted with.

- Specific designs on throw pillows to be used around the house.

- Designs on flower vases, baskets, and other materials in and around the house.

- Customized flower vases that can be given as gifts or used to spice up the living quarters.

- Vinyl-covered dressers and closet chests, etc.

DIY Projects Involving Stenciling

Stenciling is one of the kinds of projects you can embark upon using the Cricut machine. With this machine, you can design your stencils with which the designs will be made, after which you can make use of the stencils to produce on any surface the systems you have cut out. Some of the projects you can embark upon using these stencils include

- Stenciled sandbox cover.

- Basket labels created by stenciling.

- Stenciled designs on the walls, etc.

Label Designing

Cricut designing is not only left for more complicated and bigger pieces of DIY crafts. Even things as minute-seeming as labels can be created using these machines, and the beauty of it is that the owner of the design gets to choose and do whatever he wants with the design at hand.

This way, he has autonomy over what the label will come out looking like.

There are a lot of opportunities that exist under this category, including;

- Labeling of kitchen utensil jars.

- Image-labeled toy bins.

- Battery kits that hold different battery types.

- Garden stakes.

- Magnetic basket labels, etc.

Woodwork

As we said earlier, even the thicker materials, including wood, do not get to be left out of the fun. The Cricut machine can be used to create a lot out of the right piece of wood, and depending on the creativity levels of the artist, there are basically no limits to what can be achieved using these machines and given the right kinds of wood. However, if working with wood is going to be successful, be sure to refer to the guide which your device came with. This is so that you can see the limit of the width of materials your Cricut can cut through. If you ignore this, you will feed the wrong kind of material through your machine, and the result will not be good. Here are a few woodwork ideas you can engage in.

- Branding of designs on wood. This can be achieved by programming what system you want to be made on the wood into the design space of your machine and getting the device to do the job of cutting. With this in mind, feel free to go to town and create anything you can think of.

- Wall designs made from wood fillings and small pieces of wood that have been cut and branded using the machines. With these, you can create beautiful patterns to make your house look more comfortable and lived-in.

These, in no way, represent all that you can possibly achieve using the Cricut machine you have. They are only ideas that should form the basis of all that you do. Feel free to draw inspiration from these ideas that have been discussed and see what you can come up with. Remember, there are other materials you can design with, including vinyl and even paper. Let these stimulate you into releasing your inner genius.

CHAPTER 6:

Project for Beginners

Projects to Start Off With

1. Vinyl Decals and Stickers

One of the projects you can carry out with the Cricut Maker is the cutting of vinyl and stickers.

2. Fabric Cuts

The presence of the Rotary Blade in the Cricut Maker makes it a well-respected machine. The Maker can cut any type of fabric, including; chiffon, denim, silk, and even heavy canvas. With this machine, you can cut vast amounts of materials without using any backup, and this is because it comes equipped with a fabric cutting mat. Awesome machine!

3. Sewing Patterns

One significant benefit of owning the Cricut Maker machine is the extensive library of sewing patterns that you'll have access to. The library has hundreds of patterns, including some from Riley Blake Designs and Simplicity; all you need to do is select the way you want, and the machine will do the cutting.

4. Balsa Wood Cuts

The Knife Blade, coupled with the 4kg force of the machine means that the Cricut Maker can easily cut through thick materials (up to 2.4mm thick). With these features, thick materials that were off-limits for earlier Cricut Machines are now being done.

5. Thick Leather Cuts

Just like Balsa wood, the Cricut Maker is also used for thick leather cuts.

6. Homemade Cards

Paper crafters use the Cricut Maker because the power and precision of the machine make the cutting of cards and paper far quicker and more comfortable. With the device, homemade cards just got better.

7. Jigsaw Puzzles

With the Cricut Maker, crafters can make jigsaw puzzles because the Knife Blade cuts through much thicker materials than ever before.

8. Christmas Tree Ornaments

Cricut machine owners can easily make Christmas tree ornaments. All you have to do is to go through the sewing library for Christmas patterns, use any fabric of your choice to cut out the pattern, and sew them together.

Remember, the Rotary blade cuts through all sorts of fabric.

9. Quilts

Thanks to the partnership between Cricut and Riley Blake Designs, Cricut Design Space now has several quilting patterns in the sewing pattern gallery. The Cricut Maker is now used to cut quilting pieces with high precision before they are sewn together.

10. Felt Dolls and Soft Toys

The "felt doll and clothes" pattern is one of the simplest designs in the sewing pattern library. Thus, it is used for homemade dolls and toys.

The process is easy; just select the pattern you want, cut, and then sew.

11. T-Shirt Transfers

The Cricut Maker is used for cutting out heat transfer vinyl for crafters to transfer their designs to fabric. To achieve this, you have to make your design in Design Space, load the machine with your heat transfer vinyl, cut the material, and then iron the transfer onto the t-shirt. Alternatively, you can use the Cricut Easy Press to transfer the vinyl.

12. Baby Clothes

The Cricut Maker cannot cut adult clothing patterns because the mat size is only 12'x24. However, you can easily make baby clothing patterns with the machine.

13. Doll Clothes

Just like baby clothes, the Cricut Maker can easily make doll clothing patterns because the mat size is big enough.

14. Fabric Appliques

The bonded fabric blade doesn't come with the Cricut Maker, but if you buy it, you will be able to use your machine to cut intricate fabric designs like appliqué. For the bonded fabric blade to cut effectively, there has to be clicked backing on the material.

15. Calligraphy Signs

The stand out feature of the Cricut Maker is the Adaptive Tool System. With this feature, the machine will remain relevant in the foreseeable future because it fits with all the blades and tools of the explore series, as well as all future blades and tools made by Cricut.

The Calligraphy pen is one of such tools, and it is ideal for making signs and cards.

16. Jewelry Making

For crafters that like to explore jewelry making, the power of the Cricut Maker means that you can make thicker materials, and while you can cut things like diamonds, silver, or gold, you can try to make a beautiful pair of leather earrings.

17. Wedding Invitations and Save the Dates

Weddings are capital intensive, and we all know how the so-called 'little' expenses like STDs and invitation can add up to the huge cost. However, if you have the Cricut Maker machine, then you can make your invitation and STDs yourself.

The Maker is capable of making invitations of the highest quality. It cuts out intricate paper designs, and the calligraphy pen is very useful too.

18. Wedding Menus, Place Cards, and Favor Tags

The Cricut Maker is not restricted to the production of pre-wedding Invitations and STDs.

With the machine, you can also produce other items such as place cards, wedding menus, and favor tags, etc.

To keep the theme front and center, the crafter is advised to use a similar design for all their stationery.

19. Coloring Book

With the Cricut Maker, you can make 'mindful coloring' books from scratch. To achieve this goal, you need a card, paper, and a beautiful design.

Then you command the Cricut Maker to create your personal and unique coloring book with the aid of the Fine-Point Pen tool.

20. Coasters

In the sewing library, there are some beautiful coaster patterns, and as such, the Maker is used to coasters.

With the Cricut Machine, you can work with materials such as metallic sheets, quilt, leather, and everything in between.

21. Fabric Keyrings

The Cricut Maker makes fabric keyrings, and the process is simple – It cuts out the pattern and then sews it together. Besides, there are many designs for fabric keyrings in the sewing pattern library.

22. Headbands and Hair Decorations

The Cricut Maker is known to cut through materials like thick leather, and this has gone on to inspire the production of intricate headbands and hair decorations. The machine is so inspiring; crafters in the fashion world use it for creative designs and projects.

23. Cut-Out Christmas Tree

It is a typical tradition for people to buy Christmas trees during the holiday season. However, if you don't have enough space for a big tree in your living room, or maybe you're allergic to pine, then you can create your own Christmas tree. The production of an interlocking wooden tree is something the Cricut Maker does easily because the blade is capable of cutting through thick materials like wood. With the Cricut Maker, no laser is used.

24. Cake Toppers

When Cricut bought over the Cake cutter machine, the idea was to create shapes made of gum paste, fondant, and others, etc.

The Cricut Maker can't cut as well as the Cake machine, however, it can be used to produce tiny and intricate paper designs that can be used to decorate cakes.

25. Fridge Magnets

Cricut machines like the Maker and Explore air are capable of cutting out magnetic materials. Thus, crafters can use the Maker to make those fancy magnetic designs placed on refrigerators.

26. Window Decals

If you're one of those that love to display inspiring quotes on your window or even `fancy little patterns on your car, then the Maker got you covered.

 You just have to load the Maker with window cling and get your design created.

27. Scrapbooking Embellishments

The Cricut Maker is used for embellishments when scrapbooking. It is public knowledge that Cricut machines are super when it comes to cutting intricate designs.

However, the Cricut Maker takes it to a whole new level, and the responsive new blades take away all forms of complexity.

28. Craft Foam Cuts

In the past, Cricut machines found it challenging to cut craft foam (especially the Explore Machines), however, the Cricut Maker, with the 4kg of force cuts through craft foam very easily.

29. Boxes and 3D Shapes

The Cricut Machines comes with a Scoring Stylus, and this tool can create items with the sharpest edges imaginable.

We all know that the Cricut Maker can execute all kinds of sewing patterns thrown at it. It can also cut paper crafts, including 3D shapes and boxes.

30. Stencils

The Maker comes in handy for people that create things that are used to create other items. The machine is incredible for making stencils, bearing in mind that you can utilize thicker materials to complete the stencils.

31. Temporary Tattoos

If you're one of those people that want to have tattoos, but don't want them permanent for life, then the Cricut Maker is your go-to machine.

With the Cricut Maker, you can etch your design on a tattoo paper (mostly coated with transfer film) and use it on your skin.

32. Washi Tape

Crafters that use Washi tape for scrapbooking can testify to how expensive it can be, especially when buying in bulk from craft stores. However, those that own the Cricut Machine can use it to cut out Washi sheets – they can print and cut their designs on it.

33. Addressed Envelopes

The Cricut Maker is an astounding machine that can save you from spending on certain items. Remember we talked about making handmade wedding invitations; with the Cricut Machine, you can also make envelopes to go with the cards.

Another good feature about the machine is that it is equipped with a Calligraphy pen and a Fine-point pen, meaning that it is capable of addressing your envelopes automatically. All you need to do is to make sure that the words are clear enough for the postman to read.

34. Glassware Decals

With a Cricut Maker, you can cut vinyl to make glassware designs. People that host themed parties will love this one, e.g., if you're hosting a summer house party and you're serving mojitos, then you can decorate your drinking glasses with coconuts and palm tree decals.

Also, people holding Xmas parties can design and cut themed stickers to use on their cups.

35. Decorations

There are a couple of other desktop craft machines that are used to create general household decorations, but the Cricut Maker is one of the best – If not the very best.

With the Cricut Maker, you'll be empowered to create 3D wall hangings, beautiful cut-outs in the living room, and even things like signage in your closets, etc.

36. Cushion Transfers

With your Cricut Maker, you can brighten up your cushion and pillows by adding your homemade designs.

With the flocked iron-on vinyl, you can create a lovely textured cushion by using heat transfer vinyl on the Cricut Machine.

37. 3D Bouquet

The machine takes us back to the wedding theme once more.

Remember, with intuitive tools like the scoring stylus and the Fine-Point, the Cricut Maker is superbly equipped to carry out intricate papercrafts. Thus, you can introduce a touch of homemade crafts to your wedding or even create flowers to design your home, knowing that you don't have to water them.

With the Cricut Maker, you can have yourself a lovely, beautiful, and immortal bouquet.

38. Gift Tags

We all know that gift tags consume some of our money during the holiday season. However, with your Cricut Maker, you don't have to buy them anymore; you can just make your own.

39. Clutch Bags and Purses

The sewing pattern library is awesome; thus, you can make different types of full-size purses, coin purses, and clutch bags.

CHAPTER 7:

Tools and Accessories

What You Need When Using a Cricut Machine

There are many tools and accessories that go with these machines, and they can all add benefits to your projects and make your life easier. Some of them are as cheap as a single dollar, and all you have to do is shop around. You may think that it's not worth it to shop around, but the important thing that you need to know is that the time you spend looking for a better deal could end up saving you a couple of hundred dollars and leave your wallet and budget intact. This is something that will really help. In this chapter, we will go through the different tools and accessories that can go with these machines, as well as a description to help you see why you would benefit from them.

The first thing we are going to talk about is blades because there are so many different options for you to choose from. The Cricut has many different blades, and they all serve a special purpose for your machine, and it can be confusing to tell which one that you should use. In this book, we're going to explain the differences you have in the following blades.

- Engraving blade

- Wavy blade

- Debossing blade

- Perforation blade

- Scoring wheel

- Rotary blade

- Knife blade

- Bonded fabric blade

- Deep point blade

- Fine point blade

The fine point blade is a workhorse for the machine. This comes with a new Cricut machine, and you can use it for almost everything that you're going to be doing. It's gold and the blades have a white rubber covering that is new if you get them from the company itself. There are many other options that you can find out there for cheaper. However, the places to buy them cheaper might not work as well, so you will have to do your research. The blades have a forty-five-degree angle, and it is used for both series of machines.

The rotary wheel comes with the Maker, and it cuts fabric while being too sharp, so you'll need to be careful. The blade needs to be replaced quite often if you missed a lot of material, and there is a kit to change the edge. Some of the Makers, if you buy them used, won't come with this blade, and you can't buy one anywhere else, so you'll have to call the Cricut company, and they will send you one for free.

The next blades that we're going to talk about are the perforation, wavy debossing, and engraving blades. All four of these blades are new, and many people don't have them yet. They are available in full housing or a quick change tip.

The wavy blade can cut a wavy line across your projects like the scissors that came out about a decade ago to cut wavy lines into paper and were such a hit among teachers and paper crafters. The perforation blade is great for cutting dashes for tear-off issues, and the debossing blade is going to work like a scoring tool on the Explorer machine, but it goes a little deeper. The engraving blade is just going to engrave into metal and other materials, but there is an important note. There is a list as to what this can cut as far as materials that it can cut, and it's a good idea to keep checking because even though we have a master list here the company does change it from time to time, so it's good to stay on top of it.

The scoring wheel is only for the Maker, and it's almost the same as the scoring stylus for the Explore machines, but there are some differences. The blade on this is very dull, and it can also come with a double scoring blade. The scoring wheel is the first of the blades to have the quick change housing, and the bottom will pop off, and you can attach a new type of edge to it. If you have the rapid change housing, you can buy the tip for the new blades, which are a little cheaper than having to buy the whole system.

The knife blade is like having an Exacto knife that cuts leather, Balsa wood, and many more items. It is only for the Maker, and you have to calibrate this when you use it because if you don't the app will have to keep reminding you to calibrate it. You can adjust the cut pressure as well, but there's a warning that goes along with this. This is not something for a beginner to try, and it's definitely not the first thing that you should try. If you're having a problem cutting the material, don't change the settings without thinking about it first and try other ways of correcting this problem.

Cricut does not guarantee that it will cut a material, which is why we have said check their website as well to see if they've updated it or made any changes. You can also adjust the pressure of the materials but do not change the setting more than one at a time or two at a time. Another tip is to be extremely careful with the knives as you could get hurt, so make sure that you're as careful as you possibly can so that you don't hurt yourself.

So the following tools are from the Cricut company, and one of the things that you might want to get for yourself is a weeder tool. A weeder tool is one of the most essential tools that you can have because while the spatula and the tweezers that the machine can come with are beneficial. The weeding tool is necessary if you're trying to lift vinyl off of your mat. There are a lot of different tools that people can use for weeding, and they all work to raise the vinyl from the backing sheet in a safe way so that the project doesn't get ruined and your mat doesn't get ruined.

However, if you want a tool that's direct from the company itself you can use the weeder tool, or you can buy the weeder toolset because it has finer points, and it might be able to do more for you.

Some of the other popular tools that people use for weeding are a dental pick, but the handles may be uncomfortable, however, you can also use an Exacto knife, but you'll have to be very careful not to damage the project or cut yourself open. They also use an old gift card or a credit card, but, you should be aware that this might scratch the project, so you'll have to be very careful with this as well.

The next tool that we're going to talk about is the spatula. The spatula is for lifting material from the cutting mat when you don't want to worry about tearing the fabric. The spatula will take care of this by lifting the material from the mat as easily as possible, and it can also be used with a scraper tool to keep the mat clean and debris free. Cricut sells the scraper and spatula together for a very reasonable price as well.

So now that we talked about the spatula, let's talk about the scraper tool. A clean mat is essential for getting a good project done and making sure that your material isn't moving around during the cutting. The last thing you need when you are spending a lot of money on the material is to have it move halfway during the project, and then you have to start completely from the beginning, and you wasted all that money as well. Other tools remove that issue, but the scraper tool is much faster, and it ensures that you have a nice clean mat. There are different sizes, but most people prefer the extra-large as it's easier to hold, and it's faster than the smaller one, which means that it can also help get the bubbles out of your vinyl.

Extra mats are always something that is recommended because there's nothing more irritating when you're working on a project than realizing that your mats are no longer sticky. There are definite ways to re-stick your mat, and they can save you money, but just in case it is still always a good idea to have a couple of extra on hand just in case you need them. The mats do different things for different projects, such as the following.

- The pink that's for fabric is, of course, only for fabric.

- A strong grip, which is purple, would be better for thicker projects like leather, poster board, or thicker card stock.

- A standard green would be for iron-on and vinyl.

- The light blue would be for paper and card stock projects.

They also offer an essential toolset that has almost every item that we're talking about it. The toolset includes the following items.

- Tweezers

- Weeder

- Spatula

- Scraper

- Scissors

- Scoring stylus

By buying this you can cut down on a lot of money instead of buying the items individually if you just buy the set instead.

A bright pad is great for many different reasons because it makes weeding so much easier because it makes the cut lines much more visible, but if you have anything more than a simple cut, this is really going to help you out because you'll be able to see exactly where the lines are, and you could even use it for adapting patterns and tracing.

An easy press is great as well. If you're still using the iron for heat transfer vinyl, the easy press makes things so much easier than iron because there's no peeling after one or two wares, and it takes out all the guesswork of the right time and temperature as well. If you have space, you can get a real heat press for just a little bit more financially if you can afford it, but we would recommend considering a beginner heat press first, especially if you're doing anything in a big quantity or for commercial purposes.

A brayer tool is good for larger vinyl projects or working with fabric, then you should use a brayer. This fixes the problem of not fully stabilizing your material before cutting. A brayer makes the material stick to the mat but without damaging it.

A paper trimmer is super handy if you want to get a straight cut. You do not have to use scissors, and you don't have to use a ruler. As such, it makes cutting a lot easier on you, especially if you're working with vinyl.

The company also sells their own trimmer, however, there are other places that you can get a trimmer as well, and if you go with a shortcut paper trimmer, it has the option for scoring to get a perfect fold, so that maybe something that you would want to look into.

Scissors make a world of differences well. The company scissors are made with stainless steel, which creates an even cut while remaining durable, as stainless steel is one of the most durable materials that we have. The scissors are quite sharp, and they come with a micro-tip blade, which means that working on the fine details in a smaller area is easier and clean right down to the point. It also has an interchangeable colored cap, which is protective as well, which means that your scissors can be stored safely.

The tweezers are super helpful, and many people have more than one type. They usually have one for small items and one for vinyl. This tool is in the Cricut tool set, but if you want to go for something else, there are Pazzlee needle point tweezers, and these tweezers have a very sharp point, which makes them excellent for vinyl. The points are also sharp enough that they can pick fine pieces from the mat without having to use the edges or any other little trick, and they can also pick up the tiniest little scraps as well. If you don't want to get the tweezers from the company, you can actually go with this other company instead.

Pens are a big part of the Cricut world as well, and you can purchase these pens in a variety of places. However, you can use other pens as well that you can find just about anywhere and for really cheap prices as well. You will find more information about the pens that you can use in the tips chapter.

The other tools that you can get for yourself are if you find that you are a busy person and that you go to other people's houses or you go on business trips or things of that nature then you might need a tote bag to carry all of your Cricut supplies and machine. The company sells a great tote for a reasonable price that you would be able to use for your benefit and so that you will be able to keep everything organized and neat the way it needs to be. If you don't like their price point, there are actually a lot of other places that you can get a great tote as well.

You can also get rotary blades or a control knife. A control knife is basically like an Exacto knife, so you'll have to be careful with this because even though it adds precision and accuracy to your projects, you could end up cutting yourself pretty badly, so you'll have to make sure to be careful.

If you need rulers because you feel like you're not accurate enough, they have these as well, and they have all different types as well as kits that have all the tools that you need so that you don't have to buy everything individually. This is a great thing to look into so that you can see everything that you need. There are many different websites on the internet where you can find tools for your machine, and each boasts that their materials are better than the rest. Cricut offers everything that you would need on their site, and they offer very reasonable prices, but you can also do some additional searching if you feel like their stuff isn't what you would want, and you would want something else. As we've already listed examples from other companies, this will help you get an idea of what we're talking about. If you decide to get these additional tools, you'll find that your projects will be able to go a lot easier, and you'll be able to have more precision and more accuracy with them as well. Many people who like the Cricut and their company recommend getting these items for just that purpose.

CHAPTER 8:

Introduction to Design Space

Design Space Installation

You will need to have a Cricut account to install Design Space. Here's how to go about it;

1.   Visit https://design.Cricut.com/.

2.   Click on "Get Started." It is a green box at the bottom end of the page.

3.   A form will appear on the next page. Fill in your details and create a password.

4.   Read the terms and conditions of use and tick the "I accept the Cricut Terms of Use" box.

5.   If you want extra content such as tutorials, deals, and the latest information, you can accept them to be sent to your email address.

6.   After these, you can then select the "Create User ID" button.

7.   When a user account has been created, a confirmation page will appear.

8.   Further questions may be asked in a form that will appear, answer the questions accurately.

9. The option to download the Design Space software will appear. Select "Download."

10. A window will pop up after the installation is complete guiding you through the process,

11. Read and accept the terms of the agreement.

12. The software will be installed.

Getting Cricut Design Space Uninstalled

To uninstall Cricut Design Space, you follow these steps

1. Go to Control Panel on your computer

2. Go to Programs

3. Select "Uninstall Program"

4. A list of programs will appear, select Cricut Design Space and select Uninstall.

Finding Your Machine Serial Number

The serial number of your machine is usually under your machine. It is printed on a label and stuck beneath the machine. The serial number is usually 12 digits and contains both numbers and alphabets. All Cricut Makers have a serial number that begins with the alphabet Q.

Cricut Access

Cricut Access is a paid service that allows Cricut users to have access to fonts, designs, images, and ready-to-cut projects. Membership of Cricut Access comes in three categories.

The Perfect Starter Plan

This plan works well when you are sure if you want to commit long term. It starts at $9.99per month.

Annual Plan

With this plan, you pay for a year's access to the service. When you do the math, you'd see that you pay $7.99 per month – instead of $9.99. The annual charge is $95.88.

Premium Plan

This plan gives you all the benefits of the other plans. With the premium plan, you get huge discounts on fonts, images, and ready-to-cut projects. You also get free economy shopping when you buy stuff amounting to over $50. The premium plans start at $$119.88.

CHAPTER 9:

How to Use a Cricut Machine

Setting Up the Machine

First, you'll want to set up the Cricut machine. To begin, create a space for it. A craft room is the best place for this, but if you're at a loss of where to put it, I suggest setting it up in a dining room if possible. Make sure you have an outlet nearby or a reliable extension cord.

Next, read the instructions. Often, you can jump right in and begin using the equipment, but with Cricut machines, it can be very tedious. The best thing to do is to read all the materials you get with your machine – while we'll go over the setup in this book, if you're still stumped, take a look at the manual.

Make sure that you do have ample free space around the machine itself, because you will be loading mats in and out, and you'll need that little bit of wiggle room.

Now, once you have the Cricut initially set up, you'll want to learn how to use Design Space.

Using Cricut Software

So, Cricut machines use a program called Cricut Design Spaces, and you'll need to make sure that you have this downloaded and installed when you're ready. Download the app if you plan to use a smartphone or tablet, or if you're on the computer, go to http://design.cricut.com/setup to get the software. If it's not hooked up already, make sure you've got Bluetooth compatibility enabled on the device or the cord plugged in. To turn on your machine, hold the power button. You'll then go to settings, where you should see your Cricut model in Bluetooth settings. Choose that, and from there, your device will ask you to put a Bluetooth passcode in. Just make this something generic and easy to remember.

Once that's done, you can now use Design Space.

When you're in the online mode, you'll see a lot of projects that you can use. For this tutorial, I do suggest making sure that you choose an easy one, such as the "Enjoy Card" project you can get automatically.

So, you've got everything all linked up – let's move onto the first cut for this project.

Imputing Cartridges and Keypad

The first cut that you'll be doing does involve keypad input and cartridges, and these are usually done with the "Enjoy Card" project you get right away. So, once everything is set up, choose this project, and from there, you can use the tools and the accessories within the project.

You will need to set the smart dial before you get started making your projects. This is on the right side of the Explore Air 2, and it's basically the way you choose your materials. Turn the dial to whatever type of material you want, since this does help with ensuring you've got the right blade settings. There are even half settings for those in-between projects.

For example, let's say you have some light cardstock. You can choose that setting or the adjacent half setting. Once this is chosen in Design Space, your machine will automatically adjust to the correct setting.

You can also choose the fast mode, which is in the "set, load, go" area on the screen, and you can then check the position of the box under the indicator for dial position. Then, press this and make your cut. However, the fast mode is incredibly loud, so be careful.

Now, we've mentioned cartridges. While these usually aren't used in the Explore Air 2 machines anymore, they are helpful with beginner projects. To do this, once you have the Design Space software, and everything is connected, go to the hamburger menu, and you'll see an option called "ink cartridges." Press that Cricut, and from there, choose the Cricut device. The machine will then tell you to put your cartridge in. Do that, and once it's detected, it will tell you to link the cartridge.

Do remember, though, that once you link this, you can't use it with other machines – the one limit to these cartridges.

Once it's confirmed, you can go to images and click the cartridges option to find the ones that you want to make. You can filter the cartridges to figure out what you need, and you can check out your images tab for any other cartridges that are purchased or uploaded.

You can get digital cartridges, which means you buy them online and choose the images directly from your available options. They aren't physical, so there is no linking required.

Loading and Unloading Your Paper

To load paper into a Cricut machine, you'll want to make sure that the paper is at least three inches by three inches. Otherwise, it won't cut very well. You should use regular paper for this.

Now, to make this work, you need to put the paper onto the cutting mat. You should have one of those, so take it right now and remove the attached film. Put a corner of the paper to the area where you are directed to align the paper corners. From there, push the paper directly onto the cutting mat for proper adherence. Once you do that, you just load it into the machine, following the arrows. You'll want to keep the paper firmly on the mat. Press the "load paper" key that you see as you do this. If it doesn't take for some reason, press the unload paper key, and try this again until it shows up.

Now, before you do any cutting for your design, you should always have a test cut in place. Some people don't do this, but it's incredibly helpful when learning how to use a Cricut. Otherwise, you won't get the pressure correct in some cases, so get in the habit of doing it for your pieces.

CHAPTER 10:

The Basics of Cricut

Cricut Machine Basics

Cricut machines are essentially computerized gadgets operated by designers and individuals that specialize in intensive home crafting to cut out different shapes, designs, patterns, and whorls on materials. Examples of materials used for these craftworks include vinyl sheets, paper, parchment paper, wood, leather, and fabric.

A Cricut machine is a better alternative to knives, blades, saws, and every other cutting implements out there on your work table.

Why is this?

It is safer and faster. Besides, it will fetch you neater, excellent, and professional results.

You do not even need to learn the art of graphic designing before you can use a Cricut machine and make money off it! All you just need to set on the table is your creativity. With a Cricut machine, you get to craft out breath-taking designs you would never have thought to be in existence. You could even draw, embellish your plans, and create three-dimensional lines for boxes and cards.

Parts of a Cricut Machine

A Cricut machine has the following parts.

1. The adaptive system: This system is like a small in-built powerhouse that fuels your Cricut activities.

2. Blade: This is the part behind the crisp cuttings and lines your Cricut gives you. In cases where your cuttings do not come out as neat as you expected, this part might need to be changed.

3. Housing: This part holds the blade in place during cutting.

4. Cricut mats: This is a sticky platform to which you attach the material you want to cut. It is known as the backing material, and it exists in numerous colors. So, most importantly, as your Cricut device is cutting the material, this mat will help hold it in place to prevent messy jobs.

5. A polished pad: This accessory brightens your working surface. You will need it if you are a crafter of large designs that require high levels of neatness and meticulousness. It is also great for tracing images and jewelry production.

6. Brayer: It is a tool that assists you in fastening your material to the mat.

CHAPTER 11:

What Materials Can Cricut Use

There are many different materials that the machines can use for any project you desire, and we will be breaking down which machine can use what materials. Something that you should know is that there are materials that the maker can cut that the other machines cannot. Over one hundred different types of fabric, as a matter of fact. The official website of the Cricut machines does change periodically in what they say the machines can cut, and so you will need to check their website as a result of this. In doing so, you will realize what you can still cut and what may have been taken off of the list.

The explore series can only cut certain items, and we are going to list them now.

The Explore series is able to cut these items:

- Tattoo paper

- Washi tape

- Paint chips

- Wax paper

- Faux suede

- Wrapping paper

- Washi paper

- Poster board

- Parchment paper

- Sticker paper

- Construction paper

- Photo paper

- Printable fabric

- Magnetic sheets

- Paper grocery bags

- Craft foam

- Window cling vinyl

- Cardstock

- Flannel

- Vellum

- Duck cloth

- Wool felt

- Cork board

- Tissue paper

- Duct tape

- Matte vinyl

- Iron-on vinyl

- Leather up to 2.0 mm thick

- Sheet duct tape

- Oilcloth

- Soda cans

- Stencil film

- Glitter foam

- Metallic vellum

- Burlap

- Transparency film

- Chipboard that is up to 2.0 mm thick

- Aluminum metal that is up to .14 mm thick

- Stencil vinyl

- Glitter vinyl

- Glossy vinyl

- Faux-leather up to 1.0 mm thick

Fabrics, when used with the Explore series, need to be stabilized with Heat N Bond. Examples of fabrics are shown on the list below:

- Denim

- Felt

- Silk

- Polyester

Other items that the Explore Series can cut will be listed below:

- Chalkboard vinyl

- Adhesive vinyl

- Aluminum foil

- Cardboard

- Stencil film

- Dry erase vinyl

- Printable vinyl

- Outdoor vinyl

- Wood birch up to .5 mm thick

- Corrugated cardboard

- Shrink plastic

- Metallic vellum

- White core

- Rice paper

- Photo framing mat

- Pearl cardstock

- Cereal boxes

- Freezer paper

- Iron-on

- Printable iron-on

- Glitter iron-on

- Foil iron-on

- Foil embossed paper

- Neon iron-on

- Matte iron-on

The Maker can cut everything that the Explore series can cut, but it can cut so much more because the Explore series operates with three blades, but the Maker has six. The fact that they have six blades, it is able to cut more fabric and thicker fabric as well. They also differ from the Explore series because the Maker doesn't have to use Heat N Bond to stabilize fabrics. This is a great thing because it means that you can go to a fabric store and choose a fabric and use it for a project with no preparation and no additional materials either. The Maker is also able to utilize the rotary blade as well. This type of blade is new, and it differs from the others that the Explore machines use because this blade spins, and it also twists with a gliding and rolling motion. This rolling action is going to allow the Maker to cut side to side as well as up and down. Having a blade able to cut in any direction is going to help you with the ability to craft great projects. The Maker is even able to cut (up to) three layers of light cotton at the same time. This is great for projects that need uniform cuts. The Maker is also able to use the knife blade, which is a more precise option and cuts better than the others before it. This blade can cut up to 2.4 mm thick. This machine is also able to use ten times more power to cut than the others as well.

With that being said, the Maker can cut over a hundred different fabrics that others can't. We will be supplying a list of some of those fabrics below:

- Waffle cloth

- Jacquard

- Gossamer

- Khaki

- Damask

- Faille

- Heather

- Lycra

- Mesh

- Calico

- Crepe paper

- Gauze

- Interlock knit

- Grocery bag

- Acetate

- Chantilly lace

- Boucle

- Corduroy

- EVA foam

- Tweed

- Tulle

- Moleskin

- Fleece

- Jersey

- Muslin

- Jute

- Terry cloth

- Velvet

- Knits

- Muslin

Remember that this is just scratching the surface of what the Maker can cut. There are many others because the Maker is considered to be the ultimate machine and the best of the four. The Maker is also great for sewing, and there are hundreds of these projects on Design Space. Having a machine that is able to have access to these projects and the ability to cut thicker materials means that you have a machine that opens your crafting skills to a whole new level.

CHAPTER 12:

Projects and Ideas from Easy to Hard

Easy

Fancy Leather Bookmark

Personalized leather bookmarks make really nice gifts. They are also very easy to make with the Cricut.

Materials

- Cricut metallic leather

- Cricut holographic iron-on — red for a gold effect

- Purple StrongGrip mat

- Cricut Fine-Point Blade

- Weeding tool

- Pair of scissors for cutting the material to size

- Brayer or scraping tool

- Cricut Knife Blade

- Thin gold string or ribbon

Instructions

1. Cut the leather to the size you want it to be.

2. Each leather holder is approximately 2" wide by 6" high.

3. Cut the holographic paper to the size you want it to be; this will depend on the size of the font and wording you choose for the bookmark.

4. Create a new project in Design Space.

5. Select 'Shapes' from the left-hand menu.

6. Choose the square, unlock it, and set the width to 2" with a height of 6".

7. Choose a triangle from the 'Shapes' menu and set the width to 1.982" and the height to 1.931".

8. Position the triangle in the rectangle at the bottom. Make sure it is positioned evenly as this is going to create a swallowtail for the bookmark.

9. Select the circle from the shapes menu and unlock the shape. Set the width and height to 0.181".

10. Duplicate the circle shape.

11. Move one circle to the top right-hand corner of the bookmark and the other to the left. These will be the holes to put a piece of ribbon or fancy string through.

12. Align the holes and distribute them evenly by using the 'Align' function from the top menu with both circles selected.

13. Select the top left hole with the top of the rectangle and click 'Slice' in the bottom right menu.

14. Select the circle and remove it, then delete it.

15. Select the top right circle with the top of the rectangle and click 'Slice' from the bottom right menu.

16. Select the circle and remove it.

17. Select the bookmark and move it over until you see the other two circles.

18. Select the two circles and delete them.

19. Select the triangle and the bottom of the rectangle, then click 'Slice' from the bottom right-hand menu.

20. Select the first triangle, remove it, and delete it.

21. Select the second triangle, remove it, and delete it.

22. Save your project.

23. You will now have the first part of your leather bookmark ready to print.

24. Place the leather on the cutting mat and use the brayer tool or scraper tool to flatten it and stick it properly to the cutting mat.

25. Position the little rollers on the feeding bar to the left and right, so they do not run over the leather.

26. Set the dial on the Cricut to custom.

27. Load the knife blade into the second Cricut chamber.

28. In Design Space, click on "Make it."

29. Set the material to Cricut metallic leather.

30. Load the cutting board and leather into the Cricut and hit 'Go' when the Cricut is ready to cut.

31. Unload the cutting board when the Cricut is finished printing and use the spatula to cut the leather bookmark form out.

32. Use the weeding tool to remove any shapes that should not be on the bookmark.

33. Place the holographic paper on the cutting mat and put the wheels on the loading bar back into their position.

34. Create a new project in Design Space and choose a nice fancy font. Do not make it any bigger than 1.5" wide and 3" high.

35. Save the project.

36. Click on 'Make it,' and choose the correct material.

37. Mirror the image.

38. Switch the blade in the second chamber back to the fine-point blade.

39. Load the cutting board and click 'Go' when the Cricut is ready to cut.

40. Gently peel the back off the design, heat the leather, and place the name on the bookmark where you want it positioned.

41. Use the same iron-on method as the method in the "Queen B" T-shirt project above.

42. Your bookmark is now ready to use or give as a personalized gift.

Personalized Envelopes

Making personalized envelopes for those personalized greeting cards adds that extra touch.

Materials

- Envelope 5.5" by 4.25"

- Cricut pens in the color of your choice

- Green StandardGrip mat

- Spatula

Instructions

1. Create a new project in Design Space.

2. Choose the square from the 'Shapes' menu.

3. Unlock the square, set the width to 5.5" and the height to 4.25".

4. Choose 'Text' from the right-hand menu.

5. This will be the name and address the envelope will be addressed to.

6. Choose a font and size it to fit comfortably in the middle of the envelope.

7. You can choose a different color for the font.

8. Move the text box to the middle of the envelope.

9. Select the entire envelope and click 'Attach' from the bottom right-hand menu.

10. When you move the card around the screen, the address text will move with the envelope.

11. Load the envelope onto the cutting board and load it into the Cricut.

12. In Design Space, click 'Make it.'

13. Choose a material like paper.

14. Check to see if the pen color you need is loaded into the first compartment of the Cricut.

15. When the project is ready, press 'Go' and let it print.

16. Flip the card over and stick it onto the mat.

17. Use a piece of tape to stick the envelope flap down.

18. Load it into the Cricut.

19. Change the text on the envelope to a return address or 'regards from.'

20. Change the color of the pen if you want the writing in another color.

21. When you are ready, click on 'Make it.'

22. Make sure the material is set to the correct setting.

23. When you are ready, press 'Go.'

24. Once it has finished cutting, you will have a personalized envelope.

Clear Personalized Labels

Labels are fun and can be used in many ways. These labels are designed for boxes, packets, and so on.

Materials

- Cricut clear sticker paper

- High-gloss printer paper for the Inkjet printer

- Inkjet printer (check the ink cartridges)

- Spatula tool

Instructions

1. Create a new project in Design Space.

2. Choose the heart shape from the left-hand side 'Shapes' menu.

3. Select an image from the 'Images' menu on the left-hand side menu.

4. Choose a picture of a flower or search for M1525E.

5. Unlock the flower image; position it in the top left corner of the heart. Make sure it fits without any overhang.

6. Select the heart and the flower, then click on 'Weld' from the bottom right-hand menu. This ensures that the label is printed together as a unit and not in layers.

7. Select the heart and flowers once again, then click on 'Flatten' to ensure that only the outline shape of the heart is cut out.

8. Choose 'Text' from the left-hand menu, choose a font, and type the text for your label. You can choose a color for your text.

9. Unlock and move the text into position in the middle of the label.

10. Adjust the size to fit comfortably.

11. Select the heart shape and the font, then click on 'Flatten' to ensure the label is cut as a whole and not layered.

12. In order not to waste sticker paper, you will want to print as many labels as you can per sheet.

13. Choose the square shape from the 'Shapes' menu.

14. Position it on the screen, unlock the shape, and set the measurements to a width of 6" and a height of 9".

15. Move the first label into place at the top left-hand corner of the screen.

16. Select the label and 'Duplicate it.'

17. Move the second label next to the first one. Give the labels a bit of room between each other and the edges.

18. Fit as many as you can on the sheet, then save your work.

19. Fill in each of the labels with the text you want.

20. If you have space left over when your labels are positioned, you can create smaller ones.

21. You can create all different sizes of labels, patterns, and designs.

22. Make sure that all the labels are for print and are flattened.

23. Delete the background rectangle.

24. Select all the labels and then click 'Attach' from the bottom right-hand menu.

25. Click 'Make it,' and check that the design and wording are correct before clicking 'Continue.'

26. Choose the high-gloss paper option and set it to the best quality.

27. Load the sticker paper into the Inkjet printer and press 'Send to printer.'

28. Choose 'Sticker paper' for the Cricut materials.

29. Load the 'Stickers' into the Cricut and press 'Go' when it is ready to cut.

30. The Cricut will cut out the stickers so you can peel them off the backing sheet as and when you need them.

Medium

Temporary Tattoos

Temporary tattoos are a way to have a tattoo without it being permanent. They are a big hit at kids' parties, especially when they can be customized to fit the party theme.

The tattoos are also a wonderful way to learn how to create stencils for any type of project.

Note: Depending on the type of tattoo paper you choose, the tattoos can last from 2 to 7 days. Most can be removed with soap, warm water, and a sponge. Always read the tattoo paper instructions and recommendations from the manufacturer for the best results.

Materials

- Silhouette tattoo paper

- Green StandardGrip mat

- Cricut Fine-Point Blade

- Weeding tool

- Scraping tool or brayer tool

- Pair of scissors for cutting the material to size

- Inkjet printer

Instructions

1. Open a new project in Design Space.

2. Select 'Square' from the 'Shapes' menu on the left-hand side menu.

3. Change the background color to grey.

4. Unlock the square and change it to 8 ½" width and 11" length to accommodate the size of the tattoo paper.

5. Select 'Images' from the left-hand menu.

6. You can use whichever images you want to, but for this project and to learn about stencils, choose the butterfly (#M54A66) and the shark (#MF72757A).

7. Change the colors to what you want them to be. For instance, make the butterfly orange and the shark blue.

8. These two images are examples of how the Cricut cuts out stencils. The shark will cut out as the shark's outline, while the butterfly will be a more intricate cut.

9. Unlock the shark and butterfly tattoo to set them to the size you want the tattoo to be.

10. Position them on the large grey square.

11. For the text tattoo, you are going to do one as a whole text, and the next block of text will be an outline.

12. Choose 'Text' from the left-hand side menu.

13. Choose a nice font. For the project, you can try 'Stencil' that comes with the 'System' fonts.

14. Type a slogan like "I Will Not Quit."

15. Position the text box on the grey box.

16. Measure the size of the space you want the tattoo to appear on the skin.

17. Unlock the text box and set the dimensions.

18. Change the color to blue.

19. Duplicate the text box and change the color of the text to red.

20. Move the red text out of the large grey square and position it next to the box.

21. Select 'Square' from the 'Shapes' menu on the left-hand side menu.

22. Change the background color to a grey slightly darker than the background box.

23. Unlock the square, drag it over the red text box, and change the shape to cover the text box. Make the square slightly bigger than the text to allow for some cutting space.

24. In the 'Layering' panel on the right-hand side, select the red text cut.

25. From the top menu, select 'Arrange' and move the text forward.

26. Position the text box in the middle of the smaller grey box surrounding it.

27. Select both the box and the red text.

28. Right-click and select 'Slice.'

29. Select the red text, move it out of the way, then delete it.

30. Select the grey text the red text left behind, move it out of the way, and delete it.

31. Change the box's background color to blue or red.

32. Move the stenciled text onto the grey box to position it for printing and cutting.

33. Once the tattoos are in position, make sure the grey box is positioned at the top left-hand corner of Design Space. This is essential to be able to line up and cut the tattoos.

34. Delete the large grey background box.

35. Save the project.

36. Prepare the tattoo paper.

37. Silhouette tattoo paper comes with a carrier sheet and the tattoo sheet.

38. The tattoo sheet has a matte finish side and a shiny side. It is the shiny side that the tattoo images must be printed on.

39. Load the tattoo paper into the Inkjet printer.

40. Save the project.

41. Select all the tattoos on the screen.

42. On the top menu under the 'Fill' drop-down menu, select 'Print.'

43. In Design Space, click 'Make it.'

44. Mirror the images.

45. Click 'Continue.'

46. Check that 'Add Bleed' is set to on.

47. Click 'Print.'

48. Once the tattoos have been printed, remove them from the Inkjet printer and allow them to dry. Leave them for at least 10 to 15 minutes to ensure they are completely dry before moving to the next step.

49. Stick the tattoos on the green cutting mat.

50. Remove the paper backing of the carrier sheet.

51. Carefully stick the carrier sheet over the tattoo sheet.

52. Use the scraping tool to help get any bubbles or wrinkles out of the carrier sheet and smooth it over the tattoo sheet.

53. When the carrier sheet is in place, load the mat and tattoo paper into the Cricut.

54. Change the Cricut dial to custom.

55. Make sure the fine-point blade is loaded.

56. Choose 'Custom materials' and look for tattoos.

57. You will need to add extra pressure to the blade.

58. When the Cricut is ready to cut, press 'C' to cut out the tattoos.

59. When they are done, use them when needed by applying the individual tattoo facedown onto the skin.

60. Use a wet cloth on the back of the tattoo for 10 to 15 seconds.

61. Remove the back of the tattoo, and it will be transferred onto the skin.

Non-Slip Fun Socks with Heat Transfer Vinyl

Non-slip socks are quite trendy and popular. They make excellent gifts, and they are fun to make.

Materials

- Heat transfer vinyl—ThermoFlex (color of your choice)

- Green StandardGrip mat

- Cricut EasyPress or iron

- Cricut Fine-Point Blade

- Weeding tool

- Scraping tool or brayer tool

- Pair of scissors for cutting the material to size

- Pair of cotton socks

Instructions

1. Open a new project in Design Space.

2. Select 'Template' from the menu on the left-hand side.

3. Choose the 'Flip flops' template. There is not a socks template, and the flip flops give you a better idea of the sock shape.

4. Unlock the template and change it to the size dimensions of your socks.

5. Select 'Text' from the left-hand menu.

6. Change the font to a nice chunky font or one of your choosing.

7. Type "Left Foot Goes Here." Change the color to match the color of your HTV.

8. Type each word on a different line.

9. Make the font nice and big to fit in the front part of the sock just below the toes.

10. Duplicate the text and type "Right Foot Goes Here" in the second text box.

11. Save the project.

12. Click 'Make it.'

13. Mirror the image.

14. Choose the correct material.

15. Make sure that the fine-point blade is loaded.

16. Load the vinyl on the cutting mat.

17. Load the cutting mat into the Cricut and press 'C' when it is ready to cut.

18. Unload the cutting mat when it has been cut.

19. Pull the front of the vinyl off to leave the cutout shapes.

20. Use the weeding tool to clean up the letters.

21. Use the pre-heated iron or EasyPress to press the socks nice and flat.

22. Place the vinyl with the weeded design onto the socks where you want the design to be transferred to.

23. Place the heated iron or EasyPress onto the sock for 30 seconds.

24. Remove the press or iron and let it cool down.

25. While it is cooling down, do the second sock.

26. Pull the backing sheet off and your socks are done.

Party Plates

Trying to find plates to match a party theme can be challenging. With the Cricut, you can make your own to match your theme.

Materials

- Gold Cricut foil (or color of your choice)

- Transfer tape

- Paper plates in the color of your choice

- Green StandardGrip mat

- Cricut Fine-Point Blade

- Weeding tool

- Scraping tool or brayer tool

- Pair of scissors for cutting the material to size

Instructions

1. Open a new project in Design Space.

2. Select 'Template' from the menu on the left-hand side.

3. Change the background color to match the color of your plates.

4. Unlock the shape and change it to the same dimensions of your plates.

5. Choose 'Text' from the menu on the left-hand side.

6. Type "Happy Birthday."

7. Resize the text to fit on the top of the plate.

8. Change the text color to gold and choose a font you like.

9. Choose an image you want from 'Images' or upload your own.

10. Resize it to fit beneath the "Happy birthday" and set the color to gold.

11. Select both, the text and image, right-click, and select 'Attach.'

12. Save the project.

13. Click 'Make it.'

14. You may have more than one plate to make. The cutting screen is a great place to make copies of the party plate image.

15. At the top left-hand corner of the screen, you will see 'Project copies.'

16. Next to the text, there is a scroll box with the number 1 on it.

17. For a standard-sized dinner plate, you should be able to get around 4 images per 12" by 12" cutout.

18. Set the number of project copies to 4.

19. Four copies of the design will appear on the page.

20. Position them with enough space around them for a comfortable cut. If there is room for more, increase the number of copies.

21. Check that the fine-point blade is loaded in the Cricut.

22. Set the Cricut dial to custom.

23. Cut out the foil to size and stick it to the cutting mat.

24. Load the cutting mat into the Cricut.

25. In Design Space, select the correct material.

26. When the Cricut is ready to cut, press 'Go.'

27. When the Cricut is finished cutting out the shapes, unload the mat.

28. Foil is a bit trickier than other materials to use.

29. Carefully remove the piece that is no longer needed.

30. You can gently use the weeding tool, but some tape like soft plumber's tape may work better.

31. Once you are happy with the cleaned-up image, cut them out into separate squares.

32. Use a piece of transfer tape the same size as the image square to place over the image.

33. Use the scraper or brayer tool to smooth it out and ensure there are no bubbles.

34. Pull the backing sheet off the image and stick it to the party plate.

35. Use the scraping tool or brayer tool to make sure the image is completely pressed onto the plate.

36. Gently pull off the transfer tape.

37. Your party plate is ready to use.

Hard

Leather Cuff Bracelet

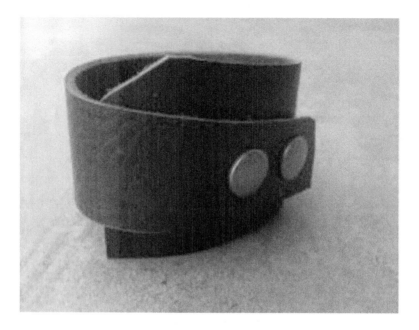

Materials

- A small piece of leather

- A bracelet or piece of chain or cord, and small jump rings

- Needle-nose pliers for jewelry

- Deep cut blade for the Cricut Explore

Instructions

1. Your first step is to choose the design image that you would like
to use on your leather bracelet. This can be found inside the
image files under Lace or any other design file that you already
have.

2. Next, verify that the sizing is appropriate for a bracelet by cutting it on paper. You definitely do not want to cut the leather and be wrong. This would waste the materials.

3. Once the size is perfect, you are able to begin your project.

4. Place the leather on the mat with the smooth side down and push the Cut button.

5. After the leather piece is cut, you will need to adjust your chain or rope to the appropriate size that is needed for the wrist of the person that it will be fitting.

6. Connect the leather to the chain with the jump rings. Attaching the links to the leather is perfectly fine, but it may tear the leather, so using the jump rings is a great alternative.

Wooden Hand-Lettered Sign

Materials

- Acrylic paint for whatever colors you would like

- Vinyl

- Cricut Explore Air 2

- Walnut hollow basswood planks

- Transfer Tape

- Scraper

- An SVG file or font that you wish to use

- Pencil

- Eraser

Instructions

1. You will need to start by deciding what you will want to draw onto the wood.

2. Then, place some lines on the plank to designate the horizontal and vertical axis for the grid. Set this aside for later.

3. Upload the file that you wish to use to the Design Space. Then cut the file with the proper setting for vinyl.

4. Weed out the writing or design spaces that are not meant to go on the wood.

5. Using the transfer tape, apply the tape to the top of the vinyl and smooth it out. Using the scraper and the corner of the transfer paper, slowly peel the backing off a bit at a time. Do it carefully.

6. Remove the backing of the vinyl pieces, aligning the lettering or design so that it is fully centered. Place it carefully on the wooden plank.

7. Again, use the scraper to smooth out the vinyl on the plank.

8. Take off the transfer tape by smoothing off the bubbles as you scrape the wood sign. Discard the transfer tape at that time.

9. Continue to use the scraper to make the vinyl smoother. There should be no bumps since this creates bleeding.

10. Now, paint your wood plank with any color of your choice. Peel the vinyl letters off. Once the paint has completely dried, you are able to erase your pencil marks.

11. As I mentioned above, these are just some of the hundreds of projects you can do with your Cricut machines. There are still many project ideas out there. On the other hand, it can be creative enough to design a project of inspiration. Some people create these projects, and nothing is stopping you from inventing new trades. The only limits exist in your mind.

Fabric & Clothing Application Projects

Tassels

Materials

- 12" x 18" fabric rectangles

- Fabric mat

- Glue gun

Instructions

1. Open Cricut Design Space and create a new project.

2. Select the "Image" button in the lower left-hand corner and search "tassel."

3. Select the image of a rectangle with lines on each side and click "Insert."

4. Place the fabric on the cutting mat.

5. Send the design to the Cricut.

6. Remove the fabric from the mat, saving the extra square.

7. Place the fabric face down and begin rolling tightly, starting on the uncut side. Untangle the fringe as needed.

8. Use some of the scrap fabric and a hot glue gun to secure the tassel at the top.

9. Decorate whatever you want with your new tassels!

Monogrammed Drawstring Bag

Materials

- Two matching rectangles of fabric

- Needle and thread

- Ribbon

- Heat transfer vinyl

- Cricut EasyPress or iron

- Cutting mat

- Weeding tool or pick

Instructions

1. Open Cricut Design Space and create a new project.

2. Select the "Image" button in the lower left-hand corner and search "monogram."

3. Select the monogram of your choice and click "Insert."

4. Place the iron-on material shiny liner side down on the cutting mat.

5. Send the design to the Cricut.

6. Use the weeding tool or pick to remove excess material.

7. Remove the monogram from the mat.

8. Center the monogram on your fabric, then move it a couple of inches down so that it won't be folded up when the ribbon is drawn.

9. Iron the design onto the fabric.

10. Place the two rectangles together, with the outer side of the fabric facing inward.

11. Sew around the edges, leaving a seam allowance. Leave the top open and stop a couple of inches down from the top.

12. Fold the top of the bag down until you reach your stitches.

13. Sew along the bottom of the folded edge, leaving the sides open.

14. Turn the bag right side out.

15. Thread the ribbon through the loop around the top of the bag.

16. Use your new drawstring bag to carry what you need!

Paw Print Socks

Materials

- Socks

- Heat transfer vinyl

- Cutting mat

- Scrap cardboard

- Weeding tool or pick

- Cricut EasyPress or iron

Instructions

1. Open Cricut Design Space and create a new project.

2. Select the "Image" button in the lower left-hand corner and search "paw prints."

3. Select the paw prints of your choice and click "Insert."

4. Place the iron-on material on the mat.

5. Send the design to the Cricut.

6. Use the weeding tool or pick to remove excess material.

7. Remove the material from the mat.

8. Fit the scrap cardboard inside of the socks.

9. Place the iron-on material on the bottom of the socks.

10. Use the EasyPress to adhere it to the iron-on material.

11. After cooling, remove the cardboard from the socks.

12. Wear your cute paw print socks!

Night Sky Pillow

Materials

- Black, dark blue, or dark purple fabric

- Heat transfer vinyl in gold or silver

- Cutting mat

- Polyester batting

- Weeding tool or pick

- Cricut EasyPress

Instructions

1. Decide the shape you want for your pillow and cut two matching shapes out of the fabric.

2. Open Cricut Design Space and create a new project.

3. Select the "Image" button in the lower left-hand corner and search "stars."

4. Select the stars of your choice and click "Insert."

5. Place the iron-on material on the mat.

6. Send the design to the Cricut.

7. Use the weeding tool or pick to remove excess material.

8. Remove the material from the mat.

9. Place the iron-on material on the fabric.

10. Use the EasyPress to adhere it to the iron-on material.

11. Sew the two fabric pieces together, leaving allowance for a seam and a small space open.

12. Fill the pillow with polyester batting through the small open space.

13. Sew the pillow shut.

14. Cuddle up to your starry pillow!

Clutch Purse

Materials

- Two fabrics, one for the exterior and one for the interior

- Fusible fleece

- Fabric cutting mat

- D-ring

- Sew-on snap

- Lace

- Zipper

- Sewing machine

- Fabric scissors

- Keychain or charm of your choice Instructions

Instructions

1. Open Cricut Design Space and create a new project.

2. Select the "Image" button in the lower left-hand corner and search for "essential wallet."

3. Select the essential wallet template and click "Insert."

4. Place the fabric on the mat.

5. Send the design to the Cricut.

6. Remove the fabric from the mat.

7. Attach the fusible fleecing to the wrong side of the exterior fabric.

8. Attach lace to the edges of the exterior fabric.

9. Assemble the D-ring strap.

10. Place the D-ring onto the strap and sew into place.

11. Fold the pocket pieces wrong side out over the top of the zipper and sew them into place.

12. Fold the pocket's wrong side in and sew the sides.

13. Sew the snap in the pocket.

14. Lay the pocket on the right side of the main fabric lining so that the corners of the pocket's bottom are behind the curved edges of the lining fabric. Sew the lining piece to the zipper tape.

15. Fold the lining behind the pocket and iron in place.

16. Sew on the other side of the snap.

17. Trim the zipper so that it's not overhanging the edge.

18. Sew the two pocket layers to the exterior fabric across the bottom.

19. Sew around all of the layers.

20. Trim the edges with fabric scissors.

21. Turn the clutch almost completely inside out and sew the opening closed.

22. Turn the clutch inside out and press the corners into place.

23. Attach your charm or keychain to the zipper.

24. Carry your new clutch wherever you need it!

Custom Graphic T-Shirt: Dinosaur T-Shirt

Everyone loves dinosaurs, and kids can't have enough t-shirts. Use iron-on vinyl to create the perfect shirt for your fossil-loving child! The small designs on the sleeves add a little extra, bringing it up a level from your standard graphic t-shirt. Just as with the rest of these projects, you can use the same idea with different designs. Customize a shirt for any of your child's interests. The Cricut EasyPress or iron will help you attach the vinyl designs to the t-shirt. You can use the Cricut Explore One, Cricut Explore Air 2, or Cricut Maker for this project.

Materials

- T-shirt of your choice

- Green heat transfer vinyl

- Cricut EasyPress or iron

- Cutting mat

- Weeding tool or pick

Instructions

1. Open Cricut Design Space.

2. Select the "Image" button in the lower left-hand corner and search "dinosaur."

3. Choose your favorite dinosaur and click "Insert."

4. Select "Image" again and search for "fossils."

5. Choose your favorite fossil and click "Insert."

6. Copy the fossil once so that you have two of them.

7. Place your vinyl on the cutting mat.

8. Send the design to your Cricut.

9. Use a weeding tool or pick to remove the excess vinyl from the design.

10. Place the dinosaur in the center of the t-shirt, and a fossil on each sleeve, with the plastic side up.

11. Carefully iron on the design.

12. After cooling, peel away the plastic by rolling it.

13. Show off the cool dinosaur t-shirt!

CHAPTER 13:

Advanced Tips and Tricks: What You Need to Know

C ricut machines are pretty straightforward with what you need to do in order to make simple designs, but you might wonder about some of the more complex operations. Here, we'll tell you how to accomplish these with just a few simple button presses.

Tips and Techniques

Blade Navigation and Calibration

The blades that come with a Cricut machine are important to understand, and you will need to calibrate your blades every single time you use your machine.

Each blade needs this because it will help you figure out which level of depth and pressure your cut needs to be. Typically, each blade needs to be calibrated only once, which is great, because then you don't have to spend time doing this each time. Once you've done it once, it will stay calibrated, but if you decide to change the housings of the blades or if you use them in another machine, you'll need to calibrate it again.

So, if you plan on using a knife blade and then a rotary blade, you'll want to make sure that you do recalibrate – and make sure you do this before you start with your project. It is actually incredibly easy to do this though, which is why it's encouraged.

To calibrate a blade, you just launch the Design Space, and from there, you open the menu and choose calibration.

Then, choose the blade that you're going to put in. For the purpose of this explanation, let's say you're using a knife blade.

Put that blade in the clamp B area and do a test cut, such as with copy paper into the mat, and then load that into the machine. Press continue, then press the go button on the machine. It will then do everything that you need for the item itself, and it will start to cut.

You can then choose which calibration is best for your blade, but usually, the first one is good enough. You can do this with every blade you use, and every time you use a new blade on your machine, I highly recommend you do this – for best results, of course.

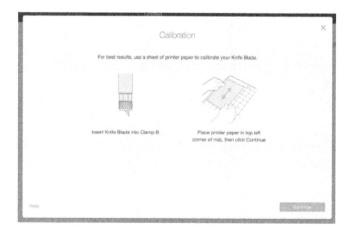

Set Paper Size

Setting paper size in a Cricut machine is actually pretty simple. You will want to use this with either cartridge or with Design Space for what you'd like to make. This also comes with a cutting mat, and you'll want to load this up with paper so that you can use it.

To do this, you'll want to make sure that you have it plugged in, then go to the project preview screen. If you choose a material that's bigger than the mat size, it will automatically be changed, and it'll be adjusted as necessary based on the size of the material that you select.

You can choose the color, the size of the material, whether or not it'll mirror – and you can also choose to fully skip the mat, too, if you don't want that image printed just yet.

Note that the material size menu does offer sizes that are bigger than the largest mat available.

If you're planning on using the print then cut mode, do understand that it's limited to a print area of 8.5x11 inches, but again, you can choose these settings for yourself.

Load Last

To load that paper and image last is pretty simple., press that, and then go. You'll be able to skip this quite easily. It's one of those operations that's definitely a little different from what you may be used to, but if you want to skip design and don't want to work with it just yet, this is probably the best option for you to use. If you're worried about forgetting it, don't worry–Cricut will remind you.

Paper Saver

Saving paper is something you'll want to consider doing with a Cricut machine because it loves to eat up the paper before you even start decorating. The Explore Air 2 definitely will appreciate it if you save paper, and there are a few ways to do so.

The first one is, of course, to halve your mats. But you don't need to do only that.

You can also go to the material saver option on the machine, which will automatically adjust and align your paper as best it can. Unfortunately, on newer machines, it's actually not directly stated, but there is a way to save paper on these.

You'll want to create tabbed dividers to organize your projects and save them directly there.

The first step is to create a background shape. Make sure that the paper looks like a background. Go to shapes and then select the square to make the square shape.

Next, once you've created squares to represent the paper, arrange this to move to the back so that the shapes are organized to save the most space on each mat. Then organize the items that are on top of where the background is and arrange them, so they all fit on a singular mat.

Rotating is your best friend – you can use this feature whenever you choose objects, so I do suggest getting familiarized with it.

Next, you hide the background at this point, and you do this by choosing the square, and in Design Space, literally hiding this on the right side. Look at the eyeball on the screen, and you'll see a line through the eyeball. That means it's hidden.

Check over everything and fine-tune it at this point. Make sure they're grouped around one object and make sure everything has measurements. Move these around if they're outside of the measurements required.

Once they're confirmed, you attach these on the right-hand side of Design Space, which keeps everything neatly together – they're all cut from the same sheet.

From here, repeat this until everything is neatly attached. It will save your paper, but will it save you time? That's debatable, of course.

Speed Dial

So, the speed dial typically comes into play when you're setting the pressure and speed. Fast mode is one of the options available on the Explore Air 2 and the Maker machines, making the machine run considerably faster than other models. You can use this with vinyl, cardstock, and iron-on materials. To set this, go to the cut screen. You'll have a lot of speed dials here and various settings. If you have the right material in place when choosing it, you'll be given the option to do it quickly with fast mode. From there, you simply tap or click on that switch to toggle this to the position for on. That will activate fast mode for that item.

It will make everything about two times faster, which means that if you're making complex swirl designs, it will take 30 seconds instead of the 73-second average it usually takes.

However, one downside to this is that because it's so fast, it will sometimes make the cuts less precise – you'll want to move back to the regular mode for finer work.

This is all usually set with the smart-set dial, which will offer the right settings for you to get the best cuts that you can on any material you're using. Essentially, this dial eliminates you having to check the pressure on this manually. To change the speed and pressure for a particular material that isn't already determined with the preset settings, you will need to select custom mode and choose what you want to create. Of course, the smart-set dial is better for the Cricut products and mats. If you notice that the blade is cutting too deep or not deep enough, there is a half-settings option on each material that you can adjust to achieve the ideal cut. Usually, the way you do this with the pre-set settings is to upload and create a project, press "go", load the mat, and then move the smart-set dial on the machine itself to any setting. Let's select custom and choose the speed for this one. In Design Space, you choose the material, add the custom speed, and adjust these settings. You can even adjust the number of times you want the cut to be changed with the smart-set dial, too. Speed is something you can adjust to suit the material, which can be helpful if you're struggling with putting together some good settings for your items.

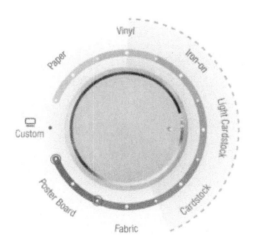

Pressure Dial

Now, let's talk about pressure. Each piece of material will require different pressure settings. If you're not using enough pressure, the blade won't cut into the material, and if you use too much pressure, you'll end up cutting the mat, which isn't what you want to do. The smart-set dial kind of takes the guesswork out of it. You simply choose the setting that best fits your material, and from there, you let it cut. If you notice you're not getting a deep enough cut, then you'll want to adjust it about half a setting to get a better result. From there, adjust as needed. But did you know that you can change the pressure on the smart-set dial for custom materials? Let's say you're cutting something that's very different, such as foil, and you want to set the pressure to be incredibly light so that the foil doesn't get shredded. What you do is you load the material in, and you choose the custom setting. You can then choose the material you plan to cut, such as foil – and if it's not on the list, you can add it.

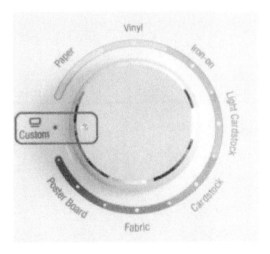

From here, you're given pressure options. Often, people will go too heavy with their custom settings, so I do suggest that you go lighter for the first time and change it as needed. There are a number of draggers that goes from low to high. If you need lots of pressure, obviously let it go higher. If you don't need much pressure, make sure it's left lower. You will also want to adjust the number of times the cut is done on a multi-cut feature item. This is a way for you to achieve multiple cuts for the item, which can be incredibly helpful for those who are trying to get the right cut or if the material is incredibly hard to cut. I don't suggest using this for very flimsy and thin material, because it'll just waste your blade and the mat itself.

That's all there is to it! This is a great way to improve on your Cricut designs. Personally, I love to work with custom cuts, and you can always delete these if you feel like they don't work. You just press the change settings button to adjust your pressure, speed, or how many cuts you want, and then choose to save when you're done.

What if you don't like a setting, period? You can delete it, of course!

To delete, go to materials settings, and you'll see a little trash can next to it. Press the trash can, and the setting will be removed.

Adjusting the pressure and cuts is part of why people love using Design Space, and it's a great feature to try.

Cricut Vocabulary, Tips, Tricks, and Keyboard Shortcuts

Now that you are more familiar with Design Space and the Cricut machines, you may have come across a few terms you were not familiar with.

Cricut Vocabulary

When working with the Cricut cutting machines and Design Space, you are going to come across different terminology. The following is a glossary of the Cricut vocabulary to help you better understand the system. The following are general Cricut terminology, as "Design Space" terminology was covered at the beginning of the book.

Backing

The backing is the back sheet of material such as vinyl. It is the part of the material that gets stuck onto the cutting mat and is usually the last part of the material to be removed after cutting, weeding, and transfer of the project.

Bleed

The bleed refers to a space around each item to be cut. This gives the cutting machine the ability to make a more precise cut. It is a small border that separates cutting items on a page. This option can be turned off, but it is not recommended.

Bonded Fabric

Bonded fabric is a material that is not very elastic, it is held together with adhesive and is not typical woven type fabric.

Blade

Cricut has a few different types of cutting blades and tips. Each blade has its own unique function enabling it to cut various materials.

Blade Housing

The blade housing is the cylindrical tube that holds the blade and fits into the blade head and blade accessory compartment of the Cricut cutting machine.

Blank

Cricut offers items, called blanks, to use with various projects for vinyl, iron-on, heat transfer vinyl, or infusible ink. These items include T-shirts, tote bags, coasters, and baby onesies.

Brayer

The Brayer is a tool that looks a bit like a lint roller brush. It is used to flatten and stick material or objects down smoothly as it irons out bubbles, creases, etc.

Bright Pad

A Bright Pad is a device that looks like a tablet. This device has a strong backlight to light up materials to help with weeding and defining intricate cuts. It is a very handy tool to have and can be used for other DIY projects as well.

Butcher Paper

Butcher paper is the white paper that comes with the Cricut Infusible Inks sheets.

It is used to act as a barrier between the EasyPress or iron when transferring the ink sheet onto a blank or item.

Carriage

The carriage is the bar in the Cricut cutting machine which the blade moves across.

Cartridge

Cartridges are what the older models of the Cricut cutting machine used to cut images.

Each cartridge would hold a set of images. They can still be used with the Cricut Explore Air 2, which has a docking site for them. If you want to use them with a Cricut Maker, you will have to buy the USB adaptor. Design Space still supports the use of Cartridge images.

Cartridges also come in a digital format.

Cricut Maker Adaptive Tool System

The Cricut Maker comes with an advanced tools system control using intricate brass gears. These new tools have been designed to aid the machine in making precise cuts and being able to cut more materials such as wood, metal, and leather.

Cut Lines

These are the lines along which the cutting machine will cut out the project's shapes.

Cutting Mat

There are a few different types of cutting mats, also known as machine mats. Most of the large mats can be used on both the Cricut Explore Air 2 and the Cricut Maker. The Cricut Joy needs mats that are designed specifically for it.

Cut Screen

When you are creating projects in Design Space, there is a green button on the top right-hand corner of the screen called the Make it button. When the project is ready to be cut, this button is clicked on. Once that button has been clicked, the user is taken to another screen where they will see how the project is going to be cut out. This is the Cut Screen.

Drive Housing

The Drive Housing is different from the Blade Housing in that it has a gold wheel at the top of the blade. These blades can only be used with the Cricut Maker cutting machine.

EasyPress

A Cricut EasyPress is a handheld pressing iron that is used for iron-on, heat transfer vinyl (HTV), and infusible ink. The EasyPress' latest models are the EasyPress 2 and the EasyPress Mini.

EasyPress Mat

There are a few different EasyPress Mat sizes that are available on the market. These mats make transferring iron-on, heat transfer vinyl, and infusible ink a lot simpler. These mats should be used for these applications instead of an ironing board to ensure the project's success.

Firmware

Firmware is a software patch, update, or newly added functionality for a device. For cutting machines it would be new drivers updates, cutting functionality, and so on.

Design Space software, Cricut cutting machines, and Cricut EasyPress 2 machines need to have their Firmware updated regularly.

Go Button

This can also be called the "Cut" button. This is the button on the Cricut cutting or EasyPress machine that has the green Cricut "C" on it. It is the button that is pressed when a project is ready to be cut or pressed for the EasyPress models.

JPG File

A JPG file is a common form of digital image. These image files can be uploaded for use with a Design Space project.

Kiss Cut

When the cutting machine cuts through the material but not the material backing sheet it is called a Kiss Cut.

Libraries

Libraries are lists of images, fonts, or projects that have been uploaded by the user or maintained by Cricut Design Space.

PNG File

A PNG file is another form of a graphics (image) file. It is most commonly used in Web-based graphics for line drawings, small graphic/icon images, and text.

Ready to Make Projects

Design Space contains ready to make projects, which are projects that have already been designed. All the user has to do is choose the project to load in Design Space, get the material ready, and then Make it to cut the design out. These projects can be customized as well.

Scraper Tool

The Scraper tool comes in small and large. It is used to make sure that the material sticks firmly to a cutting mat, object, or transfer sheet.

Self-Healing Mat

Cricut has many handy accessories and tools to help with a person's crafting. One of these handy tools is the Self-Healing Mat. This mat is not for use in a cutting machine but can be used with handheld slicing tools to cut material to exact specifications

SVG File

The SVG file format is the most common format for graphic files in Cricut Design Space. This is because these files can be manipulated without losing their quality.

Transfer Sheet/Paper

A transfer sheet or transfer paper is a sheet that is usually clear and has a sticky side.

These sheets are used to transfer various materials like transfer vinyl, sticker sheets, and so on onto an item.

Weeding/Reverse Weeding

Weeding is the process of removing vinyl or material from a cut pattern or design that has been left behind after removing the excess material. For example, weeding the middle of the letter "O" to leave the middle of it hollow.

Reverse Weeding would be leaving the middle of the letter "O" behind and removing the outside of it.

Weeding Tool

The Weeding tool has a small hooked head with a sharp point. This tool is used to pick off the material that is not needed on a cut.

For instance, when cutting out the letter 'O' the weeding tool is used to remove the middle of the letter so that it is hollow.

Cleaning up a cut design with the Weeding tool is called weeding.

Keyboard Shortcuts

The following are a few useful keyboard shortcuts that can be used in Design Space:

Copy — Ctrl+C

Paste — Ctrl+V

Cut — Shift+Delete

Undo — Ctrl+Z

A Few Design Space Tips

Here are a few handy tips for Navigating Design Space:

Color Sync Panel

To quickly and accurately match up object colors or cut down on material colors, use the Color Sync Panel. This panel is also handy to use for exactly matching non-standard colors.

Search Bar

When searching for Images, Fonts, or Projects, you will get more choices if you clearly define your search. For instance, if you are searching for Roses, leave off the 's' and search for Rose instead. If you are searching for elephants, choose the Animal or Wildlife categories and then search for elephants.

Canvas Workspace

To change the look of the Workspace without using the Main menu setting options, click in the blank space between the X and Y axis ruler at the top left-hand corner of the page. This will reset the Grid.

Save Most Used Materials

Instead of searching through hundreds of Material options when you are ready to cut out the design, add your most-used materials to Favorites.

Use Selected Objects Functions

When you select an object on the Workspace screen or the Prepare screen, you'll notice a box surrounding the selected item. The box will have icons on either all four box corners or two of the box corners. Those are quick shortcut keys for Delete, Rotate, Move, Hide, Size, and Unlock an object.

CHAPTER 14:

How to Clean Your Cricut Device

The final thing to keep clean is the actual Cricut Cutter machine. The machine needs to be wiped down with a damp cloth. Only wipe down the external panels of the machine and with the machine unplugged. Always wipe down the machine with a dry cloth after cleaning the outside of the machine. Never clean the Cricut Cutter machine with abrasive cleaners such as acetone, benzene, and all other alcohol-based cleaners. Abrasive cleaning tools should never be used on the Cricut Cutter machine either. Also, never submerge any component of the machine or the Cricut Cutter machine into the water as it can damage the machine. Always keep the Cricut Cutter machine away from all foods, liquids, pets, and children. Keep the Cricut Cutter machine in a very dry and dust-free environment. Finally, do not put the Cricut Cutter machine in excessive heat, excessive cold, sunlight, or any area where the plastic or any other components on the Cricut Cutter machine can melt.

Cleaning and Care

Cleaning your machine is very important, and you should do it regularly to keep everything in tip-top shape. If you don't take care of your machine, that's just money down the drain.

But What Can You Do To Care For Your Machine?

Be gentle with your machine. Remember, it is a machine, so you'll want to make sure that you do take some time and try to keep it nice and in order. Don't be rough with it, and when working with the machine parts, don't be too rough with them, either.

Caring for your machine isn't just about making sure that the parts don't get dirty, but you should also make sure that you keep everything in good working order.

Ensure Your Machine Is On Stable Footing

This may seem pretty basic, but ensuring that your machine is on a level surface will allow it to make more precise cuts every single time. The rocking of the machine or wobbling could cause unstable results in your projects.

Ensure no debris has gotten stuck under the feet of your machine that could cause instability before proceeding to the next troubleshooting step!

Redo All Cable Connections

So your connections are in the best possible working order, undo all your cable connections, blow into the ports or use canned air, and then securely plug everything back into the right ports. This will help to make sure all the connections are talking to each other where they should be!

Completely Dust And Clean Your Machine

Your little Cricut works hard for you! Return the favor by making sure you're not allowing gunk, dust, grime, or debris to build up in the surfaces and crevices. Adhesive can build up on the machine around the mat input and on the rollers, so be sure to focus on those areas!

Check Your Blade Housing

Sometimes debris and leavings from your materials can build up inside the housings for your blades! Open them up and clear any built-up materials that could be impeding swiveling or motion.

Sharpen Your Blades

A very popular Cricut trick in use is to stick a clean, fresh piece of foil to your Cricut mat and run it through with the blade you wish to sharpen. Running the blades through the thin metal helps to revitalize their edges and give them a little extra staying power until it's time to buy replacements.

Cleaning the Machine Itself

In general, the exterior is pretty easy to clean – you just need a damp cloth. Make sure that you never put any machine components in water.

Always disconnect the power before cleaning, as you would with any machine. Sometimes, grease can build up – you may notice this on the cartridge bar if you use cartridges a lot.

Greasing the Machine

If you need to grease your machine, first make sure that it's turned off and the smart carriage is moved to the left. Use a tissue to wipe this down, and then move it to the right, repeating the process.

From there, move the carriage to the center and open up a lubrication package. Put a small amount onto a Q-tip.

Never use spray cleaner directly on the machine, for obvious reasons. The bar holding the housing shouldn't be wiped down, but if you do notice excessive grease, please take the time to make sure that it's cleaned up. Remember to never touch the gear chain near the back of this unit, either, and never clean with the machine on for your own safety.

Cricut machines are great, but you need to take care in making sure that you keep everything in rightful order.

Conclusion

Thank you for making it to the end. Cricut machines are awesome gadgets to own because they do not only boost creativity and productivity, they can also be used to create crafts for business. With Design Space, crafters can create almost anything and even customize their products to bear their imprints.

All over the world, people use these machines to make gift items, t-shirts, interior décor, and many other crafts, to beautify their homes, share with friends and family during holidays, and even sell, etc.

There two types of Cricut machines; the Cricut Explore and the Cricut Maker. Both machines are highly efficient in their rights, and experts in the crafting world make use of them to create a plethora of items, either as a hobby or for business.

Both machines are similar in many ways, i.e., the Cricut Maker and the Explore Air 2, but the Cricut Maker is somewhat of a more advanced machine because it comes with some advanced features, as compared to the Explore Air 2.

One distinct feature about the Maker that sets it apart from the Explore Air is the fact that it can cut thicker materials. With the Maker, the possibilities are limitless, and crafters can embark on projects that were never possible with Cricut machines before the release of the Make.

Another feature that puts the Cricut Maker machine ahead of the Explore Air 2 is the 'Adaptive Tool System.' With this tool, the Cricut Maker has been empowered in such a way that it will remain relevant for many years to come because it will be compatible with new blades and other accessories that Cricut will release in the foreseeable future.

Although both machines have several dissimilarities, there are also areas where they completely inseparable. Let's take for example the designing of projects in Cricut Design Space.

Take note that the Cricut Design Space is the software where all the magnificent designs are made before they are sent to be cut. It is one of the most important aspects in the creation of crafts in the Cricut set up. However, when it comes to Cricut Maker and the Explore Air 2, there is nothing to separate them in this regard, because both machines use the same software for project design.

Cricut Design Space comes with some exciting tools and features that can make crafting easy and straightforward. These tools are not so hard to use, thus, in order to get conversant with them, you need to do some research and consistently apply the knowledge you gain from your research and reading. Expert crafters know all about the important tools in Cricut Design Space, as well as the role they play in the design of projects. Some of these tools include; the slice tool, weld tool, contour tool, attach tool and flatten tool, etc.

Cricut machines do not function separately when you purchase them; they come with accessories and tools that are required for them to function. Minus the tools and accessories that come in the pack, there are also others that can be purchased separately in order to boost the machine's functionality and output. In this book, we have discussed the basic accessories and tools that are needed for crafters to use along with their machines for optimum functionality and ease of design and production.

There are so many amazing things that you can do with a Cricut machine. This book is only the beginning of what your creativity can do if you work with the Cricut machine. There are only new and better updates that are happening to the machine, so now is the best time to get one and get in the door to understanding what all it can do for you. We hope that the information we have provided you on what materials you can use with the machine, how to get your first project started, and all the project ideas are the tools you need to achieve the goals that you have with the Cricut machine.

Printed in Great Britain
by Amazon

74074578R00081